HERMENEUTICS AND REFLECTIC T0324527

Heidegger and Husserl on the Concept
of Phenomenology

Friedrich-Wilhelm von Herrmann is known as a major figure in phenomenological and hermeneutics research: he was Martin Heidegger's
personal assistant for the last ten years of Heidegger's life, and assistant
to Eugen Fink, who in turn was primary assistant to Edmund Husserl. However, von Herrmann's own philosophical commentaries and
readings of Heidegger's work are not familiar to many in the English-
speaking world.

Von Herrmann's *Hermeneutics and Reflection*, translated here from the
original German, is the most fundamental and critical reflection on the
concept of phenomenology as it was used by Heidegger and by Husserl. It provides a careful review of Husserl's essential contribution to
phenomenology, and then draws a clear demarcation between Husserl's reflective phenomenology and Heidegger's hermeneutic phenomenology. While showing the fullest respect for Husserl's approach,
Hermeneutics and Reflection offers a full-fledged critique of Husserl from
the perspective of Heidegger's hermeneutic phenomenology.

(New Studies in Phenomenology and Hermeneutics)

FRIEDRICH-WILHELM VON HERRMANN is an emeritus professor of philosophy
at Albert-Ludwigs-Universität Freiburg.

KENNETH MALY is an emeritus professor of philosophy and environmental
studies at the University of Wisconsin–La Crosse.

New Studies in Phenomenology and Hermeneutics

Kenneth Maly, General Editor

New Studies in Phenomenology and Hermeneutics aims to open up new approaches to classical issues in phenomenology and hermeneutics. Thus its intentions are the following: to further the work of Edmund Husserl, Maurice Merleau-Ponty, and Martin Heidegger – as well as that of Paul Ricoeur, Hans-Georg Gadamer, and Emmanuel Levinas; to enhance phenomenological thinking today by means of insightful interpretations of texts in phenomenology as they inform current issues in philosophical study; to inquire into the role of interpretation in phenomenological thinking; to take seriously Husserl's term *phenomenology* as "a science which is intended to supply the basic instrument for a rigorously scientific philosophy and, in its consequent application, to make possible a methodical reform of all the sciences"; to take up Heidegger's claim that "what is own to phenomenology, as a philosophical 'direction,' does not rest in being *real*. Higher than reality stands *possibility*. Understanding phenomenology consists solely in grasping it as possibility"; and to practise *phenomenology* as "under way," as "the *praxis* of the self-showing of the matter for thinking," as "entering into the movement of enactment-thinking."

The commitment of this book series is also to provide English translations of significant works from other languages. In summary, **New Studies in Phenomenology and Hermeneutics** intends to provide a forum for a full and fresh thinking and rethinking of the way of phenomenology and interpretive phenomenology, that is, hermeneutics.

For a list of books published in the series, see page 153.

Hermeneutics and Reflection

*Heidegger and Husserl on
the Concept of Phenomenology*

FRIEDRICH-WILHELM VON HERRMANN

Translated by Kenneth Maly

UNIVERSITY OF TORONTO PRESS
Toronto   Buffalo   London

Published in German as *Hermeneutik und Reflexion. Der Begriff der Phänomenologie bei Heidegger und Husserl* © 2000 by Vittorio Klostermann, Frankfurt am Main
English Translation © University of Toronto Press 2013
Toronto Buffalo London
www.utorontopress.com

Reprinted in paperback 2022

ISBN 978-1-4426-4009-2 (cloth)
ISBN 978-1-4875-4764-6 (paper)

Publication cataloguing information is available from Library and Archives Canada.

We wish to acknowledge the land on which the University of Toronto Press operates. This land is the traditional territory of the Wendat, the Anishnaabeg, the Haudenosaunee, the Métis, and the Mississaugas of the Credit First Nation.

University of Toronto Press acknowledges the financial support of the Government of Canada, the Canada Council for the Arts, and the Ontario Arts Council, an agency of the Government of Ontario, for its publishing activities.

**Canada Council
for the Arts**   **Conseil des Arts
du Canada**

Funded by the   Financé par le
Government   gouvernement
of Canada   du Canada

ONTARIO ARTS COUNCIL
CONSEIL DES ARTS DE L'ONTARIO
an Ontario government agency
un organisme du gouvernement de l'Ontario

Canada

For Gerhart Baumann,
With gratitude,
In honour of his 80th birthday.

Contents

Translator's Introduction

This "Translator's Introduction" has five parts:

I. Putting von Herrmann's text in context
II. Issues specific to this translation, including an annotated glossary
III. Bibliography and footnote apparatus
IV. Technical aspects of the text in translation
V. Acknowledgments

I. Putting von Herrmann's Text in Context

If we start from the perspective of von Herrmann's overall contributions to Heidegger-thinking, we have to focus primarily on his interpretations and elucidations of *Sein und Zeit* and his intensive work of interpretation and elucidation of *Beiträge zur Philosophie (Vom Ereignis)*. Regarding the first, his three hefty volumes *Hermeneutische Phänomenologie des Daseins* provide the most extensive and in-depth reading and interpretation of Heidegger's first major work. Regarding the second, his book *Wege ins Ereignis. Zu Heideggers "Beiträge zur Philosophie,"* along with his many essays on being-historical thinking, provide one of the most stalwart and reliable readings and rereadings of Heidegger's second major work.

Having been blessed with a close working relationship with Eugen Fink (from whom he gained first-hand and deep knowledge of Husserl's life-work) and with Martin Heidegger (with whom he worked closely during the latter years of Heidegger's life), von Herrmann is perhaps the best-situated philosopher to offer insight into the work of these thinkers, including Husserl's reflective phenomenology and Heidegger's hermeneutic phenomenology. Indeed, it is this wisdom and knowledge that von Herrmann gives us in the translation presented here, *Hermeneutics and Reflection: Heidegger and Husserl on the Concept of Phenomenology.*

His extensive publications and his many seminars, lecture courses, and presentations are an indication that von Herrmann's own contributions to phenomenological philosophy are more than external commentaries on Heidegger's thought. For this reason, von Herrmann eschews commenting *on* Heidegger and then dividing his thinking into "periods" in the history of philosophy.

What is commentary that is not "mere" commentary, thus not standing outside the pathway of thinking that it is commenting on? What is interpretation that is not mere exegesis (i.e., interpretation of texts), that is, merely "about" the matter at hand? Von Herrmann sometimes calls his work *Erläuterung* or "elucidation." He calls *Erläuterung* an *Auslegung*: a laying out, or *interpretation.*

What is it about von Herrmann's interpretations that cannot be reduced to an exegesis or "interpretation" that is merely "about" the matter of thinking? In *Was heißt Denken?* Heidegger says that "every translation is already interpretation [*Auslegung*]." And what drives and sustains this interpretation? Heidegger immediately says: "Every interpretation must already have entered into the said, into the issue that comes to language in what is said."[1]

Heidegger sees the kind of interpreting that stays outside the matter of thinking as "historiographical [*historisch*] presentation of some work or other," as "comparing and calculating the opinion or view [*Auffassung*] ... or exploiting the view in order to 'correct' it" – and he says that this kind of interpreting "has not grasped anything at all."[2] Rather, the interpretation has to comprehend and co-enact the same pathway of thinking. It must *stay with* the matters that are being interpreted, in such a way that, in co-enacting the thinking, it opens up possibility (the futural). Addressing the question of how to read his posthumous

---

1 Heidegger, *Was Heißt Denken?*, GA 8, 178; EA (Tübingen: Niemeyer, 1954), 107; ET of EA, *What Is Called Thinking?*, trans. J. Glenn Gray (New York: Harper & Row, 1968), 174. For an explanation of these and all other abbreviations in the footnotes, see pages xxvi–xxix of this Translator's Introduction.

2 Heidegger, *Besinnung*, GA 66 (Frankfurt am Main: Klostermann, 1997), 421; ET *Mindfulness*, trans. P. Emad and T. Kalary (London and New York: Continuum, 2006), 372.

works – i.e., how to "interpret" them – Heidegger says that they have to have "deep within, the power of *letting-ahead* – [the power] of the ground-breaking grasping-ahead for an entirely other, very long questioning." A few sentences later he says that what is needed is *"the dynamics of raising the only question."*[3]

This is the manner of interpretation that takes place in von Herrmann's works: interpretation that co-enacts the thinking in the text is interpreted – interpretation that has already entered into what is said and the bearings that come to language therein. Interpretation is the phenomenological enactment of the same pathway that the original text has traversed. This leads naturally to the outcome that translation, too, is a phenomenological enactment of the same and in the same way.

This interpretation as phenomenological enactment of the same pathway of thinking brings the question of the original into the same region of questioning – and thus goes beyond mere commentary, to interpretation that evokes the same matter for thinking that inheres in Heidegger's original text. Von Herrmann's reading of the text opens up this matter for thinking.

The interpreter is not the same as the original thinker. But the interpreter is called upon to inhabit the same crucible where thinking in the original dwells. Thus the work of interpretation is also a work of thinking. As is the translation, although on yet another level.

Let me now outline what are the most significant contributions to thinking that von Herrmann's deep interpretation provides. I quite intentionally do not distinguish here between "content" and "approach" or "way of thinking."

1. This text outlines and unfolds an intensive encounter and engagement with Husserl and Heidegger. This includes a careful rendition of Husserl's essential contribution to phenomenology as well as the distinction between Husserl's reflective phenomenology and Heidegger's hermeneutic phenomenology. In the process, it offers a clear picture of how Heidegger's phenomenology differs from that of Husserl.
2. This text points to the essential meaning of primordial science and its relation to the "return to the things themselves," to hermeneutic

---

3 Ibid., 428; ET, 378.

phenomenology, and to the things of an a-theoretical nature. Thus primordial science has to do with a-theoretical *life*.

3. Granting how important Husserl's ground-breaking work in phenomenology was for Heidegger, this text shows how Heidegger's own opening to hermeneutic phenomenology reveals the demand "to break the domination of the theoretical"[4] in philosophy up until now.

4. The perceived thing is that whose significance is founded either on reflective consciousness (Husserl's reflective phenomenology) or on the founding character of the lived experience of the surrounding world, without any foundation in a corporeal world and without the primacy of reflective consciousness. Founding the thing on this lived experience is what is called for in Heidegger's hermeneutic phenomenology.

5. Theoretical reflective phenomenology involves an I-pole that is distinct from the lived-experience and from which judgment or cognition of what is takes place. By contrast, "a-theoretical" phenomenology deals with lived-experience that does not belong to an I-pole. Rather, the I is an I that experiences the world, an I that is intricately involved with lived-experiences, an I that is "historical" and engaged, over against a detached and theoretical I.

6. Following this notion of a separate I-pole belonging to reflective phenomenology, von Herrmann clarifies and summarizes what reflective phenomenology wants: "Reflection is thus characterized by the fact that we place ourselves outside the enactment of the lived-experience and the being-given-over to what is experienced that belongs to it – and then bend back to living-experience and thereby make this into the intentional object of the reflecting act."[5]

7. Von Herrmann distinguishes the idea of scientific knowledge and its primacy from the scientific character of encountering beings themselves, directly and immediately: "what is primary in phenomenological philosophy dare not be a preconceived idea of scientific knowledge ... what is *primary* is rather that *things are able to freely present themselves*, which first traces out the character of scientificality."[6]

---

4 Von Herrmann, *Hermeneutics and Reflection*, 17.
5 See ibid., 68.
6 See ibid., 103.

8. This text, as well as all of von Herrmann's texts, exhibits the highest precision of reading and interpreting a text, for the sake of and from within the self-showing of "the things themselves."

9. Von Herrmann is careful to give all possible respect and credit to Husserl for (a) opening the pathway of phenomenology and the possibility for Heidegger to carry the thinking of phenomenology in the direction that he did and (b) providing a way of access to the things themselves that is "true" and "valid" in its own right – even as this "truth" and "validity" of Husserl's reflective phenomenology challenges us to think carefully the meaning of these words, given the clear demarcation that von Herrmann sees in Heidegger's phenomenology and that he tries to interpret and give expression to in this text.

10. Von Herrmann makes clear, here and in many places, that his own hermeneutic phenomenology is bound within the pathway of thinking that Heidegger opened up. This being-tied-to-the-pathway is another way of saying how deep interpretation goes along with the thinking and *enacts* the same thinking as the original, as well as opening thinking to possibility. This enactment belongs to a reading of the text that allows for this opening. The language used may be different and the direction taken may emphasize differently. But the enactment of thinking in this interpretation keeps within the same *Sache* and matter for thinking as the original thinking.

11. It is the power of this work, herewith presented in English translation, that von Herrmann shows the fullest respect for Husserl's contributions to phenomenology while offering a full-fledged critique of that phenomenology – while showing, if you will, its "deficiency," that is, what it does *not* take into account. This juxtaposition, which seems paradoxical, underscores the power of von Herrmann's thinking to stay within this paradox – and let the matter for thinking open up, in all its possibility.

12. Given all of the above, von Herrmann's way of interpreting these early texts of Heidegger – and opening up possibility in them – sets the highest of standards by which the myriad "commentaries" and "interpretations" of *Sein und Zeit* and *Beiträge zur Philosophie* (*Vom Ereignis*) are to be measured. For certain, von Herrmann's interpretation of Heidegger cannot be simply imagined away. It is indispensable.

II. Issues Specific to This Translation, including an Annotated Glossary

> ... *the difficulty of a translation is never a merely technical one, but rather*
> *it has to do with the human relationship to what belongs to the word*
> *as its own and to the dignity of language.*[7]

Given the way in which language works for Heidegger, Husserl, and von Herrmann, each philosopher's language has a unique character. Also, von Herrmann's text mirrors and works with the texts and language of Heidegger and Husserl, and this is manifest in the ways of language as they are enacted by him in his text. Each of these three philosophers achieves a breakthrough in language that mirrors a breakthrough in his thinking. One could say that for Husserl and for Heidegger – and for von Herrmann – the work of thinking enters new territory and that the language of each carries and shows that thinking. And the translator must heed this dimension of the language.

This is not the place for a detailed "philosophy of translation" as itself a philosophical matter.[8] It is clear to everyone that there is no objective standard when it comes to the work of translation. Nor is there a universal method to apply to this work.

---

7 Heidegger, *Hölderlins Hymne "Der Ister,"* GA 53 (Frankfurt am Main: Klostermann, 1984), 76; ET *Hölderlin's Hymn "The Ister,"* trans. W. McNeill and J. Davis (Bloomington: Indiana University Press, 1996), 64.

8 For a thoughtful reflection on the core issues of translating Heidegger that I find most useful, I refer the reader to the following essays: Parvis Emad, "Thinking More Deeply into the Question of Translation: Essential Translation and the Unfolding of Language," in *Reading Heidegger: Commemorations,* ed. John Sallis (Bloomington: Indiana University Press, 1993), 323–40; F.-W. von Herrmann, "*Übersetzung als philosophisches Problem,*" in his book *Wege ins Ereignis: Zu Heideggers "Beiträgen zur Philosophie"* (Frankfurt am Main: Klostermann, 1994), 307–23. For a careful reading and interpretation of this essay, see chapter 5, "What Translation Calls for, Philosophically," in my book *Heidegger's Possibility: Language, Emergence – Saying Be-ing* (Toronto: University of Toronto Press, 2008), 69–82. See also my essay "Reticence and Resonance in the Work of Translating," in B. Babich, ed., *Festschrift for William J. Richardson* (Dordrecht: Kluwer Verlag, 1995), 148–56. For an astute description and working through of the relation between intralingual and interlingual translation *in practice,* see Parvis Emad, "Translating Heidegger's *Contributions to Philosophy* as a Hermeneutic Responsibility," in his book *On the Way to Heidegger's Contributions to Philosophy* (Madison: University of Wisconsin Press, 2007), 21–42.

The mystery of translation is that it *is*, that it *works*, and that it *plays with us* – while all the while what is deeply own to language and translation remains impenetrable.

Here I might add that, although dictionaries are vital to the work of translating, they are by no means sufficient or adequate. They do not provide all the English words that are needed for a rich but difficult philosophical text.

Given the many challenges that face the translator, let me share here some of the key issues for translating von Herrmann's text:

1. *Husserl's terminology.* There is a generally accepted standard for translating Husserlian terms into English. It is the *Guide for Translating Husserl* by Dorion Cairns.[9] For those terms in von Herrmann's text that are clearly demarcated as belonging to the Husserl-discourse, I have used this *Guide* most of the time. In some cases, where the English word suggested by Cairns is awkward – and where there seems to be an alternative – I have deviated from the *Guide*. For the German *vergegenwärtigen* I have used "making-present" rather than "presentiate"; for *Vorstellung* I have used "presentation" rather than "objectivating" or "objectivating intention."

2. *Heidegger's terminology.* Since there is no similarly accepted standard for translating Heidegger into English, I have translated all Heidegger quotations into English myself. In almost all cases I have conferred with the English translations that are available, especially those of *Sein und Zeit*. The bibliographical information (see below) includes pagination that allows the reader to easily find the given text and the published translation thereof.

3. *The most problematic words for translation.* In addition to the individual word or word families that I discuss below, for the most problematic words in translation I have inserted the original German word in brackets in the translation's text. I have tried to keep this practice to a minimum but have sometimes found that putting these German words in brackets is useful, either to improve understanding of the text in general or to provide important information to the reader who is trained in phenomenology, Husserl, Heidegger, and von Herrmann.

---

9 Dorion Cairns, *Guide for Translating Husserl* (The Hague: Nijhoff, 1973).

4. An "annotated glossary": Issues relating to individual words and phrases.
Given the preceding points regarding translation and in that context,
I offer the following reflections on significant issues with individual
words. All of these words are "problematic" in one sense or other.

die Anschauung	intuition
anschauen	intuit
die Intuition	in-tuition
	[Note that the hyphenated *in-tuition* is simply to distinguish the German *Intuition* from *Anschauung*. Thus the reader knows how to interpret, depending on which technical term is used in German.]
ausführen	elaborate, carry out, execute
die Ausführung	elaboration, carrying out, execution
	[This word has two senses, one of expanding, the other of executing, enacting, carrying out.]
bedeuten	mean, signify
die Bedeutung	meaning
die Bedeutsamkeit	significance
bedeutsam	significant
	[To be distinguished from *Sinn*, which I have translated as "sense."]
das Besorgen/besorgen	care-for, concern
besorgend	concernful
die Besorgung	concern
	[Ties in with *Sorge* or "care."]
die Einstellung	setting, focus
einstellen	focus, tune
die Erkenntnis	knowledge, cognition
erkennen	know, cognize
	[When referring specifically to Husserl, I have used *cognition*

and *cognize*, to emphasize that the word in Husserl names the mental function of knowing. Otherwise, when the word is less technical, I use *knowledge* and *know*.]

das Er-lebnis	lived-experience
das Er-leben /er-leben	living-experience

[Sometimes I translate *erleben* as "experience/experiencing" when it seems to be used more generally than the key word *er-leben*. I also translate *erfahren* as "experience" – and add the German *erfahren* in brackets whenever it seems that the word is more significant than usual.]

fassen	apprehend, comprehend (Cairns adds: conceive)
erfassen	grasp (Cairns adds: seize upon)
auffassen	apprehend (Cairns adds: take, construe)

[When it is clear that the word refers to Husserl, I have tried to be consistent with Cairns. In cases where these words are less technical and do not refer specifically to Husserl, I have translated them in various ways, depending on context.]

das Leben	life, living
die Lebendigkeit	livingness
lebendig	living, livelily (adv.)
das Objekt	ob-ject
objektiviert	ob-jectified
objektivieren	ob-jectify

der Gegenstand	object
die Vergegenständlichung	objectification
	[Hyphen is used here to demarcate whether the German is *Objekt* and its cognates, or *Gegenstand* and its cognates. The hyphen could have been used vice versa.]
umgehen	go around with, deal with
der Umgang	involvement
der Vor-gang	what passes by, passing-by, process
der Prozeß	process [not an essential word in the text]
vorbeigehen	pass by
zutunhaben	deal with
beschäftigtsein	be engaged with
vergegenwärtigen	make present
die Vergegenwärtigung	making-present
das Sich-an-ihm-selbst-zeigen	self-showing-in-itself
das/ein Sich-an-ihm-selbst-zeigende/s	what-shows-itself-in-itself something-that-shows-itself-in-itself

I have distinguished between self-showing-in-itself for *Sich-an-ihm-selbst-zeigen* and something-that-shows-itself-in-itself or what-shows-itself-in-itself for *das/ein Sich-an-ihm-selbst-zeigendes*. In this reading, the latter phrase refers to "beings" and the former to "being." Thus *das/ein Sich-an-ihm-selbst-zeigende/s* names the phenomenon; and *das Sich-an-ihm-selbst-zeigen* names being, or that by virtue of which things show themselves – being as disclosure, as unconcealment, as φύσις, as ἀλήθεια.

5. Two words that call for special attention.

die Existenz	existence
existenzial	existential

Existenzial has a very specific meaning in Heidegger and *Being and Time*. It has nothing to do with and says nothing about what we normally refer to as "existentialism" and "existential." This misreading of the word has handicapped Heidegger-thinking for many decades now. Von Herrmann's elucidations here should put that misreading to rest for good.

The being of Dasein is *Existenz* – that is, the being for whom its own being is an issue. In other words, Dasein is the name for human being in the manner of a being who is open to its own being. But its own being ties in with disclosure of being or being as disclosure. So the being of Dasein, named *Existenz*, is one prong of the twofold disclosure that Dasein does and the disclosure that being is.

There are several key elements to Dasein and its being:

a. Self-related – the being who comports itself to itself as one for whom its own being is at issue.
b. Ecstatic – the being who stands out, who is open to the open expanse in which Dasein stands, that is, the open expanse of the Da.
c. Horizontal – the being who in its comportment to itself is also always already stretched to the being of beings that are ready-to-hand, to be engaged in and to be dealt with and to be gone around with – or better said: the being of beings that are engaged in, are being dealt with, and are gone around with.
d. Disclosure – the being who, in being, is open to the open expanse. *Existenz* is a relationship-with-being. Thus Dasein understands itself in its being. The disclosure that is own to being (disclosure of being and being as disclosure) to which Dasein comports itself is coupled with the disclosure that Dasein is involved in in its *Existenz* – that is, Dasein's disclosure-dynamic as being open to the way that is own to being.

Thus von Herrmann says: "We thus call the disclosure in which my own being as existence is held: the self-related-extended *disclosure*, or the *self-related-ecstatic disclosure* ... The whole of this self-related-ecstatic-horizonal disclosure of being is in essence that which Heidegger thinks in the appellation 'Dasein.'"[10]

---

10 Von Herrmann, *Hermeneutics and Reflection*, 123–4.

Note that the transformation in Heidegger's thinking between *Sein und Zeit* and *Beiträge zur Philosophie* includes a transformed way of saying what *Existenz* says in *Sein und Zeit*. In the context of be-ing-historical thinking that is at the core of *Beiträge*, Heidegger uses the German word *Inständigkeit*. If *Existenz* in *Sein und Zeit* refers to the human relation to its own being – "what is ownmost to Dasein lies in its existence" from section 9 of *Sein und Zeit* – in *Beiträge* he is naming the human comportment to being, or standing open in the open expanse of the *Da*. Thus the ecstatic character of *Existenz* mentioned above.

Turning now to be-ing-historical thinking, the word that Heidegger uses is *Inständigkeit,* or "inabiding." Inabiding is the way that humans dwell or "abide in" what is own to Dasein and to being that is named in *enowning/Ereignis* – or in being as enowning, being as disclosure, being as emergence, being as ἀλήθεια. Inabiding names the way in which humans stand in the swaying of the truth of being.

The word *Inständigkeit* does not risk being misinterpreted, even as it helps clarify the distinction between what *Existenz* says in its usual connection to existentialism and what *Existenz* says in *Sein und Zeit*, which is always already and from the very beginning *not* the existential of existentialism.

*6. The Complexity of the German word **Ereignis** or **Er-eignis** and Its Cognates **-eigen, er-eignen,** and **Eigentum.***We must distinguish clearly Heidegger's usage of these words in the 1919 text and in the texts from the 1930s. The word that is used here, in this text from 1919, is *not at all* the word that Heidegger uses in his *Beiträge zur Philosophie (Vom Ereignis)*, written between 1936 and 1938.

Von Herrmann's text focuses on *Ereignis* and its cognates in two places:

a. in the last paragraph of section 2 (pages 28–9), which focuses only on the word *Ereignis* as it is used in the 1919 text; and
b. in the final pages of section 4 (pages 46–8), where he not only expands on how *Ereignis* is meant in 1919, but also differentiates its usage in 1919 from the later and central usage of the word in the texts of the 1930s.

In the text from 1919, Heidegger's use of the word *Ereignis* wants to say two things. First, that what we are talking about here is (a) a "happening" rather than a "mere event" – isolated incident or episode – as might be known in the objective realm; this happening includes enactment, the rich dynamic of the happening as such, rather than naming a static event; and (b) the character of "own" that is said in the word element *-eigen* in the word *Er-eignis;* here the own that is named is the own of living- and lived-experience in the pre-theoretical realm of the lived-world. Rather than defining the realm by reducing it to a concept, hermeneutic thinking "enters into" the lived-experience of world in order to let what is own to it be seen and said.

In this text from 1919 the word *Ereignis* says something similar to the German word *Geschehnis:* happening. Indeed on several occasions the two words appear side by side.

At the end of section 2 von Herrmann explicates how the word *Ereignis* designates what belongs to the essential structure of lived-experience, above all of the lived-experience of the surrounding world – thus, what is "own" to that lived-experience. The word *Eigentum* names this "own" as "ownhood." We must keep in mind that this way of naming the issue keeps us from falling into the prevalent way of using these words, both in German and English: *-eigen* as "proper" and *Eigentum* as "property." Property is something that can be reified in theoretical knowing; ownhood as the essence of what is own to the dynamic of pretheoretical lived- and living-experience cannot be reified. It can only be entered into and, in understanding in looking-on phenomenologically, be understood as what is own to the dynamic enactment of lived-experience.

As regards these words in their first appearance at the end of section 2 of von Herrmann's text, I have translated *Ereignis* as "happening" and *-eigen* as "own." What is own to lived-experience is not something objectified or reifiable. Pretheoretical lived-experience does not have a property that can be theoretically known or conceptualized. What is own is the dynamic happening of lived-experience. (Note that in this section of the text von Herrmann does not use the word *Eigentum.*)

The second place where von Herrmann dwells on the word *Er-eignis* and its cognates is at the end of section 4. Here he first shows how in theoretical thinking living-experience is understood as something that passes by, to become objectified in a reflected lived-experience. This reflecting objectifying closes off the essence of lived-experiences – what is own to the dynamic, pre-theoretical enactment of lived-experiences. Thus theoretical thinking cannot enter into what is the *Er-eignis* character of lived-experience. It is merely a reflectively objectified lived-experience.

Second, hermeneutic understanding of lived-experience is "something entirely new" – that is, it has been hidden prior to Heidegger's hermeneutical understanding. For the first time the *Er-eignis* character of lived-experience is entered into. Rather than a lived-experience that passes by my theoretical understanding, I make it own to me in its essential character as lived-experience. Rather than my lived-experiences becoming the property – the usual meaning of *Eigentum* – lived experience lives from within its own, from what is own to it.

Thus *Er-eignis* of lived-experience in its pre-theoretical manifesting says what is own to this phenomenon, not a static or objectified "thing" or "standout event" but an ongoing dynamic of the enacting in question.

Given that the word *Er-eignis* points to what is own in living- and lived-experience, revealable to hermeneutic understanding and not to reflective objectifying, it becomes clear that the usage of the word *Er-eignis* in 1919 must be demarcated from the word as used in the texts of the 1930s. In von Herrmann's words (page 48): "In *Er-eignis* as essence of living and living-experience [the word used in 1919], *-eignis* has the meaning of own and ownmost; whereas, in *Er-eignis* [the word used from the 1930s onward], as the belonging-together of enowning throw [*der ereignende Zuwurf*] [to Dasein] and Da-sein's enowned throwing-open [der *ereignete Entwurf*] *-eignis*/own says as much as "ownhood [*Eigentum*]."

When von Herrmann uses the word *Eigentum* to mean "acquired lived-experiences" I translate it as "property" – its usual meaning, which then has to be abandoned in order to think the hermeneutic understanding that Heidegger has brought to the fore. When he uses the word *Eigentum* in the context of Heidegger's later being-historical thinking – where *Er-eignis* names be-ing: thus the dynamic emergence of enowning, which includes the enowning throw of be-ing, Da-sein's being enowned by that enowning throw, and Da-sein's throwing open the fullness of that unfolding-emerging-dynamic – I translate *Eigentum* as "ownhood," as a word that says the "own" within the fullness of the emergent unfolding that *is Er-eignis*. And for these moments I translate *Ereignis* as "enowning." I continue to be confident that this English word best says what Heidegger wants to say with the word *Er-eignis* in his texts from the 1930s.[11]

Whereas I could translate the word *Ereignis* from the first selection as "happening" – and whereas I can confidently translate it as "enowning" when clearly referring to Heidegger's use of the word in the 1930s – for much of the time in the second selection, von Herrmann is focusing on and working with the German word itself. And I could find no other way of "translating" *Ereignis* than leaving the word in German. I remind the reader that my decision to leave the word in German is also a "translation" and involves the interpretation that every translation is.

III. Bibliography and Footnote Apparatus

A detailed bibliography of the reflective phenomenology of Husserl and the hermeneutic phenomenology of Heidegger was prepared by von Herrmann and appears at the end of the Introduction of the translation-text (pages 8–9).

---

11 Here I acknowledge the pioneering work of the eminent Heidegger-translator Albert Hofstadter, when in 1976 he introduced the English word *enownment* as the appropriate way to bring Heidegger's word *Ereignis* into English. In the spirit of his wisdom, I stand by my decision, even as what was perfectly acceptable and appreciated in 1976 has become problematic for some Heidegger scholars today.

Let me quote from my book *Heidegger's Possibility: Language, Emergence – Saying Be-ing* (University of Toronto Press, 2008):

> Already in 1976, Heidegger scholar and translator Albert Hofstadter suggested saying Ereignis as enownment. [Albert Hofstadter, *"Enownment,"* in *Martin Heidegger and the Question of Literature: Toward a Postmodern Literary Hermeneutics*, ed. William V. Spanos (Bloomington: Indiana University Press, 1979), 17–37.] He grounded this decision in the knowledge that Heidegger wanted *ereignen* to say its connection to *eigen*: own – to make one's own, to be own to, the owning work as such. Hofstadter quotes Heidegger saying how we must simply experience this *eignen*, to experience how humans and being are 'en-owned' (*ge-eignet*) to each other. Hofstadter says *das Ereignis* is the letting-belong-together, the one befitting the other, of being and time, humans and being, the fourfold. To explain this, he states, "At the center of *das Ereignis* is *own*," and "the most literal possible translation of *das Ereignis* ... *en-, -own*, and *–ment*: *enownment* ... the letting-be-own-to-one-another ... the letting be married of any two or more ... Enownment is not their belonging, but what lets their belonging be." [p. 29]

For the "Translator's Introduction," I have placed all bibliographical information in the respective footnotes; for the translation-text itself, however, I have placed just the author and title of the work in the footnotes, along with the page reference. Full bibliographical information for both the German and the English texts is given here.

Works of Heidegger quoted in the translation-text. Unless noted otherwise, all of these texts are published by Vittorio Klostermann of Frankfurt am Main.

Abbreviations used for Heidegger-texts:

GA   *Gesamtausgabe* of Heidegger's Complete Works

EA   *Einzelausgabe* of Heidegger's works that are not a part of the *Gesamtausgabe,* that is, published individually

ET   English translation. Here the reference to the English translation will be given. Since all of the English translations of these Heidegger-texts include the German page in brackets, there are no page numbers for the ET in individual footnotes.

GA 2   *Sein und Zeit* (1927).
        Ed. Friedrich Wilhelm von Herrmann, 1977.
        EA   *Sein und Zeit* (1979).
                Max Niemeyer, Tübingen, 1979. I give both the GA and the EA pages in the footnotes.
        ET   *Being and Time.*
                Trans. John Macquarrie and Edward Robinson. New York: H&R, 1962.
                [Paperback edition, with a foreword by Taylor Carman: Harper Perennial Modern Classics, 2008.]
        ET   *Being and Time.*
                Trans. Joan Stambaugh. Albany: SUNY Press, 1996.
        ET   *Being and Time.* Trans. Joan Stambaugh. Revised and with a Foreword by Dennis J. Schmidt. Albany: SUNY Press, 2010.
                [Note that the German pagination of the EA is included in the German GA edition as well as in all English translations.]

GA 14   *Zur Sache des Denkens* (1927–1968).
        Ed. Friedrich-Wilhelm von Herrmann, 2007.

ET   *On Time and Being.* (Part I of the GA edition)
        Trans. Joan Stambaugh. New York: Harper & Row,
        1972.

GA 17   *Einführung in die phänomenologische Forschung* (1923–4).
        Ed. Friedrich-Wilhelm von Herrmann, 1994.
    ET   *Introduction to Phenomenological Research.*
        Trans. Daniel O. Dahlstrom. Bloomington: Indiana
        University Press, 2005.

GA 24   *Die Grundprobleme der Phänomenologie* (1927).
        Ed. Friedrich-Wilhelm von Herrmann, 1975.
    ET   *The Basic Problems of Phenomenology.*
        Trans. Albert Hofstadter. Bloomington: Indiana
        University Press, 1982.

GA 26   *Metaphysische Anfangsgründe der Logik im Ausgang von Leib-
        niz* (1928).
        Ed. Klaus Held, 1978, 1990 (2nd rev. ed.), 2007 (3rd rev. ed.).
    ET   *The Metaphysical Foundations of Logic.*
        Trans. Michael Heim. Bloomington: Indiana Univer-
        sity Press, 1984.

GA 56/57 *Zur Bestimmung der Philosophie* (1919).
        Ed. Bernd Heimbüchel, 1987, 1999 (rev., expanded ed.).
    ET   *Towards the Definition of Philosophy.*
        Trans. Ted Sadler. London: Continuum, 2000.

GA 63   *Ontologie. Hermeneutik der Faktizität* (1923).
        Ed. Käte Bröcker-Oltmanns, 1988.
    ET   *Ontology – The Hermeneutics of Facticity.*
        Trans. John Van Buren. Bloomington: Indiana Uni-
        versity Press, 1999.

Works of Husserl quoted in this translation-text. I will note here in this
bibliography those English translations that include the German pagination. For those works I will not give a page number for the ET in the
respective footnotes in the translation-text. In all other cases I will give
page numbers for both the German original and the English translation
in the footnotes of this translation-text.

Huss.   *Husserliana.* The Hague: Martinus Nijhoff, 1950–84.
        All bibliographical information for the volumes of *Husserli-
        ana* will appear here in the bibliography. If von Herrmann's

main reference is to an individual edition, the *Huss.* reference will come after the ET. In those cases where the only
reference is to *Husserliana*, the bibliographical information
will appear in the main entry.

ET   Here the reference to the English translation will be
     given. When the English translations include the
     German, there are no page numbers for the ET in
     individual footnotes. In all other cases I give the page
     number of the ET.

LU   *Logische Untersuchungen. Erster Band: Prolegomena zur reinen
     Logik. Zweiter Band: Untersuchungen zur Phänomenologie und
     Theorie der Erkenntnis. I. Teil (I.-V. Logische Untersuchung).
     Zweiter Band, II. Teil: (VI. Logische Untersuchung): Elemente
     einer phänomenologischen Aufklärung der Erkenntnis.* Tübin-
     gen: Niemeyer, 1968, fifth edition.

     ET   *Logical Investigations,* trans. J.N. Findlay. New York:
          Humanities Press, 1970.

     Huss. *Logische Untersuchungen. Erster Band: Prolegomena
            zur reinen Logik (Husserliana* XVIII, ed. E. Holenstein,
            1975); *Zweiter Band: Untersuchungen zur Phänomenolo-
            gie und Theorie der Erkenntnis. I. Teil (I.-V. Logische
            Untersuchung) (Husserliana* XIX/1, ed. U. Panzer
            1984); *Zweiter Band, II. Teil (VI. Logische Untersuchung):
            Elemente einer phänomenologischen Aufklärung der
            Erkenntnis (Husserliana* XIX/2, ed. U. Panzer, 1984).

Ideen *Ideen zu einer reinen Phänomenologie und phänomenologischen
       Philosophie. Erstes Buch: Allgemeine Einführung in die reine
       Phänomenologie.* Tübingen: Niemeyer, 1993, 5th ed.
       Also referred to in the text as *Ideen I.*

       ET   *Ideas Pertaining to a Pure Phenomenology and to a
            Phenomenological Philosophy, First Book: General Intro-
            duction to a Pure Phenomenology,* trans. F. Kersten, in
            Collected Works, vol. 2. The Hague: Martinus Nijhoff,
            1982. German pagination included.

       Huss. *Ideen zu einer reinen Phänomenologie und phänomenolo-
              gischen Philosophie. Erstes Buch: Allgemeine Einfüh-
              rung in die reine Phänomenologie (Husserliana* III, ed.
              K. Schuhmann, 1976).

PsW   *Philosophie als strenge Wissenschaft.* Frankfurt am Main:
      Klostermann, 1965.

ET "Philosophy as Rigorous Science," trans. M. Brain-
ard, in *The New Yearbook for Phenomenology and
Phenomenological Research,* II (2002) 249–95.

Huss. Philosophie als strenge Wissenschaft (Husserliana XXV,
Vorträge und Aufsätze (1911–21), ed. Th. Nenon and
H.-R. Sepp, 1987, 3–62).

*Krisis Die Krisis der europäischen Wissenschaften und die transzenden-
tale Phänomenologie. (Husserliana* Bd. VI, ed. W. Biemel, 1976).

ET *The Crisis of European Sciences and Transcendental Phenomenology: An Introduction to Phenomenology,* trans.
D. Carr. Evanston: Northwestern University Press,
1970.

CM Cartesianische Meditationen und Pariser Vorträge. (Husserliana
Bd. I, ed. S. Strasser, 1950).

ET *Cartesian Meditations,* trans. D. Cairns. The Hague:
Martinus Nijhoff, 1960. German pagination included.

IP Die Idee der Phänomenologie (Husserliana Bd. II, ed. W.
Biemel, 1958).

ET *The Idea of Phenomenology,* trans. W.P. Alston and
G. Nakhnikian. The Hague, Netherlands: Martinus
Nijhoff, 1966.

IV. Technical Aspects of the Text in Translation

As mentioned above, footnotes have been simplified in that not all bibliographical information appears there. Rather, it appears here in the
Translator's Introduction. Translator's notes appear in square brackets
in the footnotes.

All additions to the German text by the translator are within square
brackets [ ], including significant and problematic German words that I
have chosen to leave in the text. Parentheses within the text match what
is in the original German. The symbols { } are used to distinguish von
Herrmann's or Heidegger's additions or comments within quotations.
Numbers in square brackets [ ] refer to the pagination in the original
German text.

V. Acknowledgments

First and foremost I want to acknowledge my appreciation for the work
of F.-W. von Herrmann – in the many seminars of his that I attended in

1971–2 and 1973–6, then in the many instances over the years where he and I collaborated on translation issues and editorial work, and finally for the careful and gracious way in which he answered my questions regarding thorny issues in translating this text.

It is an honour to present this translation of one of the important texts written by F.-W. von Herrmann. His has been a lifelong dedication to phenomenology, and especially Husserl and Heidegger. His commitment to the philosophical work of editing Heidegger's texts and to his own writing, first on Heidegger, then on Husserl, then on Augustine, Descartes, Stefan George, and others, spans over five decades. He has done his work with determination, integrity, respect, and humility – and above all with grace.

This is only the second book by von Herrmann to appear in English.[12] Given that von Herrmann has authored over fifteen books and that his lifelong work is so rich, it is my hope that more translations of his books will be forthcoming.

Second, I am grateful to Gail Stenstad for agreeing to be a most precise reader and critic of my translation, and to Graeme Nicholson for his careful reading of the final manuscript.

Thirdly, I am grateful to Len Husband of the University of Toronto Press for his full support and constant encouragement, both for this translation-text and for the series New Studies in Phenomenology and Hermeneutics.

Kenneth Maly
Toronto, May 2011

---

12 The other book by von Herrmann in English is his *Augustine and the Phenomenological Question of Time*, trans. Frederick van Fleteren & Jeremiah Hackett (Lewiston: Edwin Mellen, 2008).

HERMENEUTICS AND REFLECTION

Heidegger and Husserl on the Concept
of Phenomenology

Foreword

As is clear from its subtitle, the text presented here, *Hermeneutics and Reflection*, is dedicated to the ways of phenomenology as they are tied to the names Edmund Husserl and Martin Heidegger. For one of these philosophers, it is the way of reflective phenomenology; for the other, that of hermeneutic phenomenology. This book's three chapters systematically pursue both concepts of phenomenology, but they do not present a historical development of either concept, notwithstanding that the chapters are presented in the order of their writing.

Chapter 1, "The Origin of Hermeneutic Phenomenology from within the Primordial Experience of the A-Theoretical," was written this spring [2000] specifically for publication in this book. I prepared chapter 2, "Husserl–Heidegger and 'the Things Themselves,'" in 1995, to appear the following year in *Inmitten der Zeit: Beiträge zur europäischen Gegenwartsphilosophie*, the Festschrift for Manfred Riedel's sixtieth birthday.[13] Chapter 3, "Hermeneutic Phenomenology of Dasein and Reflective Phenomenology of Consciousness," is based on a text that I published in 1981 (2nd ed. 1988, now out of print), entitled *Der Begriff der Phänomenologie in Heidegger und Husserl*.[14] For inclusion in this volume, I have deleted sections 1 and 4 and replaced them with newly prepared texts. For this volume I have reworked sections 2 and 3, which make up the core of the text.

---

13 Th. Grethlein & H. Leitner, eds., *Inmitten der Zeit: Beiträge zur europäischen Gegenwartsphilosophie* (Würzburg: Königshausen & Neumann, 1996), 276–89.

14 F.-W. von Herrmann, *Der Begriff der Phänomenologie in Heidegger and Husserl. Wissenschaft und Gegenwart. Geisteswissenschaftliche Reihe*, Nr. 63 (Frankfurt am Main: V. Klostermann, 1981, 1988²).

[2] This volume, which investigates the phenomenology of Husserl and of Heidegger, is dedicated to Freiburg's Gerhart Baumann, a specialist in German Studies, for his eightieth birthday. Early in his career, in his hermeneutic dealings with German and European poesy, Baumann took the phenomenology of Husserl and of Heidegger into account. He is among those scholars of literature who appreciate Heidegger's approach to poesy. He knew Heidegger from his courses and lectures, as well as from personal encounters, which took place primarily in conjunction with Paul Celan's visits to Freiburg. Baumann also participated in the memorable Heraclitus seminar that was directed by Heidegger and Eugen Fink at the University of Freiburg during the winter semester of 1966–7.[15] A close friendship with Eugen Fink gave him access to the rich knowledge of phenomenology that Fink had gained from being in Edmund Husserl's company every day for ten years.

I am indebted to Baumann for his unique approach to poets, an approach that I came to appreciate while I was studying German philology and over the following decades, up to the present, as I attended his many lectures in the Studium Generale of Freiburg. Beyond that, I thank him for his support of my own hermeneutic-phenomenological work at the University of Freiburg.

I am most grateful to my assistant, Professor Paola-Ludovika Coriando, for being a dialogue partner while this book was coming to fruition, as well as for her reliable help with reading proofs.

Freiburg im Breisgau, Summer of 2000

F.-W. von Herrmann

---

15 M. Heidegger & E. Fink, *Heraklit. Seminar Wintersemester 1966/67* (Frankfurt am Main: V. Klostermann, 1970); also in GA 15 *Seminare*, ed. C. Ochwadt (Frankfurt am Main: V. Klostermann, 1986, 11–266.

Introduction

"Hermeneutics and Reflection" is the perspective that will be discussed in the following investigations of the concept of phenomenology in Heidegger and in Husserl.[16] Belonging to both concepts of phenomenology is Husserl's maxim "going back to the things themselves," which Heidegger changed slightly to "to the things themselves!". The phenomenological method requires a way of doing philosophy that proceeds only from within the look of and gaze at the things themselves as they are determined in thinking. It is also what Husserl formulates as the "principle of all principles," according to which philosophy has to deal with the intuition in which the things that call for thinking are primordially given in order to take in what is primordially given, without interpolation of theoretical constructs. But already in the determination of phenomenological in-tuition there emerges a difference between Husserl's and Heidegger's understanding of phenomenology. Whereas Husserl grasps phenomenological seeing fundamentally as a reflective gaze, Heidegger marks phenomenological seeing as a hermeneutic understanding. But what is meant here by "hermeneutic" and "hermeneutics" belongs fundamentally to the task of grounding a hermeneutic phenomenology. The reflective character of phenomenological seeing also determines the factual field of investigation that manifests as consciousness. Likewise, the hermeneutic dimension that belongs to the essential character of phenomenological seeing charts the thematic field

---

16 [Translator's Note: See pages 8–9 at the end of this Introduction for von Herrmann's extensive bibliography apropos this theme.]

of the things that are to be investigated: the a-theoretical, factical life and Dasein.

Comparing and contrasting Husserl's understanding of *reflective* phenomenology with Heidegger's understanding of *hermeneutic* phenomenology takes place here by stressing three stations along the way of hermeneutic phenomenology. The *first* station is the first lecture course that the young Heidegger gave at the end of the First World War (during the war emergency semester of 1919), which was entitled "The Idea of Philosophy and the Problem of *Weltanschauung*." [4] In this programmatic lecture text Heidegger grasps and unfolds the idea of hermeneutic phenomenology and philosophy by setting it off from the reflective phenomenology of Husserl.

The *second* station along the way of hermeneutic phenomenology that is investigated here is the first Marburg lecture course (winter semester 1923–4), "Introduction to Phenomenological Research."[17] This station is emphasized because here Heidegger brings the hermeneutic phenomenology of Dasein into focus by explicitly and directly contrasting it with Husserl's own interpretation of his reflective phenomenology. In this text Heidegger indicates his appreciation for Husserl's originary phenomenological questioning and seeing in the *Logical Investigations* and his trailblazing attention to intentionality as the essential constitution of comportments (acts). At the same time, it is through Husserl's fallback on the modern position of *ego cogito* (Descartes) that Heidegger explains his own distance from the idea of phenomenology and his hermeneutic reformation of genuine phenomenological findings.

For the *third* station along the way of hermeneutic phenomenology I have chosen the section on method from *Being and Time*. In this text the unfolding of the hermeneutic-phenomenological method comes to a provisional conclusion. It is true that section 7 develops the "preliminary concept" of phenomenology, and that presentation of the fully developed "concept" of phenomenology is seen as part of the task for the part "Time and Being" – and indeed was enacted in the design of the Marburg lecture course "The Basic Problems of Phenomenology."[18] However, the section on method from *Being and Time* completely lays

---

17 Heidegger, *Einführung in die phänomenologische Forschung*, GA 17. [Please refer to pages xxvi–xxix of the Translator's Introduction for full bibliographical information for both the German and the English texts that are referenced in the footnotes.]
18 Heidegger, *Grundprobleme der Phänomenologie*, GA 24.

out the hermeneutic-phenomenological method, showing method-ological principles – type of treatment and method of access – as well as drawing out what is decisive for hermeneutics in contrast with reflection.

The title of our investigations is "Hermeneutics and Reflection," and Heidegger is mentioned first in the subtitle, followed by Husserl. Our investigations aim to clarify [5] the concept of hermeneutic phenom-enology but are mindful that this clarification is not possible without a thorough discussion of Husserl's concept of reflective phenomenology. Even so, the intention of this writing is not at all to pit Heidegger's concept of hermeneutic phenomenology against Husserl's concept of reflective phenomenology. Rather, our investigations, in which these two concepts of phenomenology face each other, are motivated by the thought that each of the two ways of phenomenology carries its own truth within it.

I would like to mention that I am filled with gratitude for the years that I spent at the University of Freiburg as assistant to Eugen Fink, per-haps *the* expert on Husserl's phenomenology. In many personal conver-sations following his lectures, I had the opportunity to partake in the rich treasury of experience that he had gathered during his decade-long daily contact with Edmund Husserl, in his capacity as Husserl's private assistant. Since Heidegger's thinking has its methodological origin in Husserl's phenomenology, any training in Heidegger's thinking cannot avoid a serious study of Husserl's phenomenological analyses. Even the late enowning-historical [*ereignisgeschichtlich*] thinking cannot deny its phenomenological and hermeneutic character. Heidegger himself witnesses to this in his text of 1936 entitled "My Way into Phenomenol-ogy" with these words: "The time of phenomenological philosophy is over. It counts as something that is past and is listed only as mere his-tory, alongside other philosophical orientations. But what is most own to phenomenology is not an orientation. It is the possibility, changing from time to time and only in this way abiding, for thinking to corre-spond [*entsprechen*] to the claim [*Anspruch*] of what calls for thinking. If phenomenology is experienced and preserved in this way, then it can disappear as title, in favor of the matter for thinking, whose revealabil-ity remains a mystery."[19]

---

19 Heidegger, "Mein Weg in die Phänomenologie," in *Zur Sache des Denkens*, GA 14, 101; ET, 82.

For Husserl's concept of reflective phenomenology, see the following:

E. Fink, *Studien zur Phänomenologie (1930–1939)* (*Phaenomenologica* vol. 21 (The Hague: Nijhoff, 1966).

L. Landgrebe, *Der Weg der Phänomenologie. Das Problem einer ursprünglichen Erfahrung* (Gütersloh: Gütersloher Verlagshaus Gerd Mohn, 1963).

W. Biemel, *Die entscheidenden Phasen der Entfaltung von Husserls Philosophie,* in *Gesammelte Schriften,* vol. 1: *Schriften zur Philosophie* (Stuttgart–Bad Cannstatt: Frommann-Holzboog, 1996).

– *Die Idee der Phänomenologie bei Husserl,* in *Gesammelte Schriften,* vol. 1: *Schriften zur Philosophie* (Stuttgart–Bad Cannstatt: Frommann-Holzboog, 1996), 147–71.

E. Ströker, *Husserls transzendentale Phanomenologie* (Frankfurt am Main: V. Klostermann, 1987).

– *Phänomenologische Studien* (Frankfurt am Main: V. Klostermann, 1987).

P. Jansen, *Edmund Husserl. Einführung in seine Phänomenologie* (Freiburg & München: K. Alber, 1976).

R. Bernet, L. Kern, & E. Marbach, *Edmund Husserl. Darstellung seines Denkens* (Hamburg: F. Meiner, 1996).

O. Pöggeler, *Die Krise des phänomenologischen Philosophiebegriffs* (1929), in *Phänomenologie im Widerstreit,* ed. Chr. Jamme, and O. Pöggeler (Frankfurt am Main: Suhrkamp, 1989), 255–76; also in O. Pöggeler, *Schritte zu einer hermeneutischen Philosophie* (Freiburg & München: K. Alber, 1994), 227–47.

For Heidegger's concept of hermeneutic phenomenology, see the following:

O. Pöggeler, *Der Denkweg Martin Heideggers* (Pfullingen: G. Neske, 1963), esp. 36 ff. & 67 ff.

– *Heideggers logische Untersuchungen.* In M. *Heidegger: Innen- und Außenansichten.* Published by the Forum für Philosophie Bad Homburg (Frankfurt am Main: Suhrkamp, 1989), 75–100; also in O.Pöggeler, *Heidegger in seiner Zeit* (München: W. Fink, 1999), 19–38.

J. Grondin, *Einführung in die philosophische Hermeneutik* (Darmstadt: Wissenschaftliche Buchgesellschaft, 1991), 119–37.

H.-G. Gadamer, *Wahrheit and Methode. Grundzüge einer philosophischen Hermeneutik. Gesammelte Werke,* vol. 1 (Tübingen: J.C.B. Mohr [Paul Siebeck], 1986), 258–75.

– *Hermeneutik,* in *Historisches Wörterbuch der Philosophie,* ed. J. Ritter (Basel & Stuttgart: Schwabe & Co., 1974), III:1066–7.

W. Biemel, *Heideggers Stellung zur Phänomenologie in der Marburger Zeit*,
in *Gesammelte Schriften*, vol. 1: *Schriften zur Philosophie* (Stuttgart–Bad
Cannstatt: Frommann Holzboog, 1996), 265–333.

F. Rodi, ed., *Vorträge gehalten auf den Symposien "Faktizität und Geschichtlichkeit"*
(13–14 June and 16–17 September 1985, in Bochum), in *Dilthey-Jahrbuch*,
IV:1986–7 (Göttingen: Vandenhoeck & Ruprecht, 1987).

Chr. Jamme, *Heideggers frühe Begründung der Hermeneutik*, in *Dilthey-Jahrbuch*,
IV:1986–7 (Göttingen: Vandenhoeck & Ruprecht, 1987).

K. Held, *Heidegger und das Prinzip der Phänomenologie*, in *Heidegger und die praktische Philosophie*, ed. Gethmann-Siefert & O. Pöggeler (Frankfurt am Main:
Suhrkamp, 1988), 111–39.

R. Thurnher, *Zu den Sachen selbst! – Zur Bestimmung der phänomenologischen
Grundmaxime bei Husserl und Heidegger*, in *Philosophie in Österreich 1996.
Vorträge des 4. Kongresses der Österreichischen Gesellschaft für Philosophie*, ed.
A. Schramm (Wien: Verlag Hölder-Pichler-Tempsky, 1996), 261–71.

M. Riedel, *Die Urstiftung der phänomenologischen Hermeneutik. Heideggers frühe
Auseinandersetzung mit Husserl*, in *Phänomenologie im Widerstreit*, ed. Chr.
Jamme and O. Pöggeler (Frankfurt am Main: Suhrkamp, 1989), 215–33.

T.S. Kalariparambil, *Das befindliche Verstehen und die Seinsfrage* (Berlin: Duncker
& Humblot, 1999), especially the chapter *"Der Durchbruch in die hermeneutische Phänomenologie: Vorlesungen von 1919–1922,"* 67–148.

E. Richter, *Heideggers Kritik am Konzept einer Phänomenologie des Bewußtseins.
Anerkennung and wachsende Distanz gegenüber dem Werk Edmund Husserls*, in
Vom Rätsel des Begriffs. Festschrift für F.-W. v. Herrmann zum 65. Geburtstag,
ed. P.-L. Coriando (Berlin: Duncker & Humblot, 1999), 7–29.

F.-W. v. Herrmann, *Hermeneutische Phänomenologie des Daseins. Eine Erläuterung
von Sein und Zeit*, vol. 1 (Frankfurt am Main: V. Klostermann, 1987), 366–74.

– *Weg and Methode. Zur hermeneutischen Phänomenologie des seinsgeschichtlichen
Denkens* (Frankfurt am Main: V. Klostermann, 1990), 15–22.

H.-H. Gander, *Selbstverständnis und Lebenswelt. Grundzüge einer phänomenologischen Hermeneutik im Ausgang von Husserl und Heidegger* (Frankfurt am
Main: V. Klostermann, 2001).

Part One

The Origin of Hermeneutic Phenomenology from within the Primordial Experience of the A-Theoretical

[11]

§ 1. Philosophy as Primordial Science, Its Originary and Ownmost Problematic, and Its Genuine Methodological Attitude for Knowledge

Heidegger's lectures from the war emergency semester of 1919, "The Idea of Philosophy and the Problem of *Weltanschauung*,"[20] programmatically outline the idea of future philosophy according to its thematic object and methodological way of proceeding. Thematically, future philosophy is grasped as pre-theoretical primordial science of the domain of pre-theoretical life and experience. According to this thematic field of investigation, the methodological way of proceeding is defined as hermeneutic phenomenology, which is likewise not of a theoretical nature, but rather an a-theoretical one. But, insofar as the theoretical is at the same time reflection, primordial science and hermeneutic phenomenology have an a-reflective character. Future philosophy is constituted precisely as pre- or a-theoretical primordial science, in its divergence from traditional philosophy, which is rooted in the theoretical. From its demarcation over against Husserl's reflective phenomenology, it is secured as a-reflective, hermeneutic phenomenology. The hermeneutic character of Heidegger's phenomenology is thus synonymous with its a-theoretical and a-reflective character.

---

20 Heidegger, *Die Idee der Philosophie und das Weltanschauungsproblem*, GA 56/57.

But what is the a- and pre-theoretical? Is it not that which philosophy and phenomenology has always known as the pre-scientific and the pre-philosophical? But then, is the passage from the pre-philosophical to the philosophical not the passage from the pre-theoretical to the theoretical? If future philosophy becomes primordial science, is it not then also theory of and reflection on the pre-theoretical? Is not all of philosophy essentially theory and reflection? Is not a pre-theoretical primordial science a contradiction in terms?

[12] These totally legitimate questions are motivated by the *prevalent* understanding of the difference between the pre-theoretical and the theoretical. However, it is precisely this dominant and "valid" difference that blocks access to the untouched domain of the pre-theoretical, with the result that this pre-theoretical has never been made visible in traditional philosophy or in reflective phenomenology. But if the domain of the a-theoretical moves into the field of vision for a seeing that is not misdirected, then this seeing and methodological opening of this domain of the pre-theoretical does not have a theoretical-reflective character, even as it is itself not a pre-philosophical, but precisely a philosophical-scientific seeing and opening.

That points to the possibility of a scientific philosophizing this side of theory and reflection. Now, theory and reflection prove to be one way, but not the only way, to investigate and enter philosophy.

The task and effort of the lectures from the war emergency semester is this first opening of the look into the domain of the a-theoretical – and then the working out of the possibility that emerges from within the insight into the a-theoretical, namely the possibility of a non-reflective, hermeneutic phenomenology.

The problem is marked in the title of the lecture course: "The Idea of Philosophy and the Problem of *Weltanschauung*." It is the idea that future philosophy needs to be redrawn as primordial science. For this idea, in contrast to philosophy up to now, *Weltanschauung* is "something totally different."[21] The task here is the "scientific circumscribing, unfolding, and partial resolution"[22] of the problem of the idea of philosophy as primordial science. "Obtaining the genuine methodological attitude for knowledge"[23] belongs to this idea of philosophy. The

---

21 Ibid., 11.
22 Ibid., 3.
23 Ibid.

methodological attitude for knowledge of philosophy as primordial science is, then, a genuine one, when it is phenomenology – but not reflective phenomenology, rather hermeneutic phenomenology.

[13] In this, we have to "step beyond and away from ourselves,"[24] beyond our naive, pre-philosophical attitude and into the philosophical attitude. Thereby, however, we have to "leave ourselves behind ... in the domain which always remains alien to the inherent problem of the science that is to be established."[25] This is the theoretical domain to which we dare not expose ourselves – as in philosophy and phenomenology up to now – by crossing over from the pre-philosophical into the philosophical attitude. Rather we have to leave the theoretical behind. This is so because the essential problematic of the primordial science that needs to be founded is the philosophical unfolding of the a- and pre-theoretical domain, which keeps itself closed off when we are theoretically oriented.

The transition from the pre-philosophical to the philosophical attitude is a "modifying calling-into-question, turning away from, and complete uncoupling from the naive consciousness of immediate life."[26] This calling-into-question, turning away from, and uncoupling have to do only with the pre-philosophical naivety of immediate life, which *as this life* needs to be made philosophically transparent, but do not have to do with the basic pre-theoretical quality of this life. This quality is obscured only when the philosophical attitude has a theoretical-reflective character. But when the philosophical attitude itself is a-theoretical, it is able to turn the a-theoretical life in its basic pre-theoretical quality around, out of its naive inarticulation into philosophical articulation. With this we get a first look into a-theoretical philosophical investigation – which is precisely not naivety but rather a philosophical opening. The modifying calling-into-question, turning away from, and uncoupling of the naive attitude to life become necessary in getting around the theoretical attitude, if the "relevance of the problem" and the "specific type of the scientific problem-area"[27] – that is, if the sphere of pre-theoretical life – is to be opened up scientifically in the primordial sense.

---

24 Ibid.
25 Ibid.
26 Ibid.
27 Ibid.

[14] *Life in its basic a-theoretical state* has already been noted as the field of investigation for philosophical primordial science. "Every Dasein with a personal life has a relationship to world, in each of its moments within its definitive, prevailing life-world."[28] A world, the life-world, belongs to every essential constitution of pre-theoretical life. Life is essentially *world-life*, the world essentially *life-world*. The relation of life to world is grasped in *Being and Time* as Dasein's being-in-the-world, the relation of life to world as existentiell world [*existentielle Welt*]. Everyone living in such and such a specific life-world has in every moment of life "a relationship to world," to the life-world, "to the values that motivate the surrounding world [*Umwelt*], to the things of its life-horizon, to fellow-humans, to society"[29] – that is, to that which, as surrounding world, as surrounding things, as co-world, as co-worldly humans, motivates and claims us in our comportment.

These "life-references"[30] to the surrounding world and the things of the surrounding world, the co-world and the co-worldly humans – all of these form, as stated in *Being and Time* (§ 9), the indifference[31] of natural-daily life (of existing), the indifferent "for now and for the most part." This indifference is not in the sense of ungenuine, but indifferent over against the different life-possibilities (difference of a definitive existing). They are the genuine life-forms of "scientific, religious, artistic, political"[32] life, which can completely dominate the natural-daily life-references.

In the idea of philosophy as primordial science of the pre-theoretical world-life and its life-world lies the "requirement" [15] "to discover a whole new concept of philosophy."[33] But refusing the philosophy of *Weltanschauung* and the questions of humanity that belong to *Weltanschauung* does not indicate some kind of retreat of future philosophy from its inherited basic questions, for a more modest philosophy of life. Future philosophy as primordial science is indeed a "catastrophe of every (previous) philosophy,"[34] but in the sense of καταστροφή, of turning

---

28 Ibid., 4.
29 Ibid.
30 Ibid.
31 Heidegger, *Sein und Zeit*, GA 2, 58; EA, 43.
32 *Die Idee der Philosophie und des Weltanschauungsproblem*, GA 56/57, 4.
33 Ibid., 11.
34 Ibid., 12.

around, of turning back from its rootedness in the theoretical and into a new rootedness in the domain of the pre-theoretical. "The cardinal question aims for the essence or concept of philosophy,"[35] "the idea of philosophy as primordial science,"[36] a new foundation of philosophy and its basic questions. Philosophical primordial science, which becomes necessary from relevant insights – and in accord with its claim to universality – stands in the tradition of πρώτη φιλοσοφία, *prima philosophia*, metaphysics, transcendental philosophy, *Wissenschaftslehre*, absolute science, and transcendental phenomenology, but with the *unfathomable difference* that these forms of philosophy have in common that they are housed in the theoretical. Primordial science, by contrast, is a philosophy from within the a-theoretical. If it succeeds in unlocking the domain of a-theoretical life as origin and support of philosophy, then it will establish the basic questions of philosophy anew on this basis.

The intention of the philosophical undertaking here is to be found in this universal reaching-out [*Ausgriff*] and not in a return to an anthropological philosophy of life. This emerges clearly from further clarifications of this undertaking. Philosophy here is "a problem as science, and that is to say: as primordial science."[37] Its future character as science becomes problematic – the insight that it achieves its ownmost character as science only by giving up [16] its previous theoretical character in favour of its pre-theoretical character. The concept of primordial science aims at something "ultimate," "having the character of a beginning," "primordial," first with reference to "the grounding and constituting."[38] Being first, it is "*principium*, a principle"[39] in relation to individual sciences, the "non-principled, *non-principium*, but derived from principle, that which issues from the source [*das Ent-sprungene*] and is not itself the source or origin [*Ur-sprung*]."[40]

In this way the primordial science we are seeking takes over the task of philosophy that began with Aristotle, namely, to provide a foundation for the individual sciences. But the source or origin from which

---

35 Ibid.
36 Ibid.
37 Ibid., 24.
38 Ibid.
39 Ibid.
40 Ibid.

the individual sciences issue is no longer the theoretical, but now for the first time the a-theoretical domain. All sciences belong to the theoretical attitude and participate in this attitude, but they emerge from an a-theoretical origin or source, which can be philosophically disclosed only pre-theoretically as this realm of source or origin. Everything depends on "methodically entering this realm of primordial science"[41] – by and in a methodical procedure that is itself a-theoretical. This a-theoretical method must itself be acquired through primordial science and its field of investigation. The intention of the lecture course of the war emergency semester is to grasp "essential components of the idea of philosophy,"[42] of the a-theoretical primordial science. But this will succeed only if in one fell swoop that methodological way of proceeding is gained that is able to open up the domain of the a-theoretical, the domain of the origin, *as* a-theoretical – and if it does not obstruct this domain by letting a theoretical approach sneak in. This methodological way of proceeding will prove to be hermeneutic phenomenology.

[17]

§ 2. The Discovery of the A- or Pre-Theoretical and the Requirement to Break the Dominance of the Theoretical

The theoretical domain spans two distinctively separate approaches to the theoretical. First, the theoretical manifests itself in scientific thinking and knowing and corresponds to the scientific. In the sciences as they are developed and put into practice, we "are met by a clearly discernible fallout of theoretical knowing."[43] The theoretical "condenses with all its might"[44] in scientific thinking. For epistemology and epistemological psychology, scientific thinking and knowing happens in "psychic processes of cognition,"[45] in psychic experiences of a specific kind, which are distinguished from the psychic experiences of pre-scientific world-experience. The theoretical way that belongs to scientific thinking and knowing is to a large extent preferred, "in the conviction that it

---

41 Ibid., 29.
42 Ibid.
43 Ibid., 59.
44 Ibid.
45 Ibid.

represents the fundamental layer"[46] that underpins the regions of pre-scientific world-experience.

Distinct from the theoretical in the sense of scientific thinking and knowledge, the theoretical in a broader, expanded sense refers precisely to the pre-scientific aspect of our scientific experiences, to the extent that all pre-scientific experiences are thematized by epistemology, philosophical psychology, and reflective phenomenology. The manner by which they thematize the life-experiences that they themselves call pre-scientific-natural is in its main outline theoretical – that is, it involves reflectively observing, making more objective, reifying, objectifying. In this second sense, the theoretical is more far-reaching and momentous than the theoretical in the narrower sense. For it is the theoretical in this second meaning that does not allow the pre-scientific experience of the world [18] to be seen in its primordiality, but rather covers this primary meaning up from the very beginning, with the theoretical method of seeing and of access.

Preference for the theoretical in the sense of scientific knowledge, and the dominance of the theoretical way of accessing the pre-scientific experience of the world, signify a *dominance of the theoretical*. "This dominance of the theoretical has to be broken."[47] Arising as it does from the usual distinction between theory and praxis, the call for revoking the dominance of the theoretical sounds as if one is granting primacy to praxis and the practical. Thus, priority would no longer be given to scientific theory, but now to action in general and specifically to moral action – that is, morals. Granted that the call for overcoming the dominance of the theoretical merely shifts priority from theory to praxis, would that already guarantee that practical action, world-experience that is related to action, is freed from the rule of its *theoretical* interpretation? Obviously not. For this distinction between theory and praxis itself belongs to the dominance of the theoretical that is meant here. Even when we shift our focus from theory to praxis, we remain under the dominance of the theoretical that has fundamentally defined traditional philosophy since its Greek origins.

The dominance of the theoretical that is part of philosophy's essence up to now must be broken, because this theoretical is first experienced as that which "points back into the pre-theoretical."[48] The significance

---

46 Ibid.
47 Ibid.
48 Ibid

of what is meant here by the theoretical and the pre-theoretical cannot be extracted from the common understanding of both. Neither the theoretical that is named here nor the pre-theoretical that is first named in the lecture text is what we already know as the difference between the scientific and the pre-scientific. This difference, for instance, as we know it [19] from Husserl's phenomenology, itself still belongs to the dominance of the theoretical. The contrast between the theoretical and the pre-theoretical that appears along the way to primordial science emerges primarily from the primordial experience of the pre-theoretical realm. With this primordial experience there manifests a sense of the theoretical that is unknown up to now, which is based on the fact that it blocks our view of the originary pre-theoretical. This pre-theoretical is precisely *not* what reflective phenomenology, for example, considers as the pre-scientific, natural world-experience. For in this view of the pre-scientific as the sense experience of the world, the primordial, pre-theoretical life of the world and the primordial, pre-theoretical life-world have already been covered over. Thus, at the beginning of the development of philosophical primordial science, we dare not associate the concepts of the pre-theoretical and the theoretical that are used here with the meanings of these words with which we are familiar. Rather we must forgo these concepts in order to stay open for the sense of what here alone, developed step by step, is meant by the pre-theoretical and the theoretical.

Additionally, since the philosophical primordial science that needs first to be drawn up speaks of experience and lived-experience and of the a-theoretical domain of lived-experience – and since, under the name of what is psychic, lived-experiences are the thematic object of psychology – we must ask what the relationship is between primordial science and psychology. The domain of lived-experience is the "*object-domain* of psychology in general."[49] Thus, we have to ask: "*What is the psychic?*"[50] If the nascent primordial science intends to make the pre-theoretical domain of lived-experience its field of investigation, may it turn to psychology, assuming that this is where the domain of lived-experience is the object-domain? In psychology, how is the psychic given as the

---

49 Ibid., 60.
50 Ibid.

"total domain"?[51] Is the psychic merely a name for the domain of lived-experience, or does this name point to the way in which psychology [20] has always already turned to the domain of lived-experience? Is there a specific way of observing the psychic that is not only psychological but also itself already primordially scientific, so that "through it [the specific way of observing] primordially scientific problems can be solved" and "objective layers of the psychic itself" can be shown, "which make up the primordially scientific object-realm"?[52] In other words, can the a-theoretical be found in the psychic, in the domain of lived-experience as a psychic one? Asked even more incisively: "If I am standing in the psychic, am I standing in the primordial domain itself? Is that where the genuine origin lies?"[53]

The answer to these questions is a definite No! For, as the psychic, the domain of lived-experience is already reified by psychology into an association of things. This reifying approach and the reflection that belongs to it have from the very beginning made the primordial, pre-theoretical domain of lived-experience invisible. As psychology puts it, the psychic is "in constant change, a network of processes going on in time, characterized precisely by temporality, thus not filling space, the domain of what is happening dissectible into elemental processes, basic facts that can then be disentangled as elemental pieces of what is (impressions, perceptions)."[54] Here it seems as if lived-experience is not available in any other way than through psychological reflection, in which it manifests itself as a processual happening in a time that is psychically immanent. But it is in and for this reflective approach that what is own to lived-experience as a-theoretical is closed off – without its ever having been sighted in its pre-theoretical character. Psychology as such, all psychology – not only psychology that is oriented and explicative of the empirical and natural-scientific, but also psychology of the social sciences, the psychology that is descriptive and analytic, as well as phenomenological-eidetic psychology – keeps to [21] the theoretical configuration and as such keeps the pre-theoretical domain of life and lived-experience closed off. From this it is already clear that the

---

51 Ibid.
52 Ibid.
53 Ibid., 60f.
54 Ibid., 61.

philosophical primordial science of life and living-experience is not the life-philosophy that is aligned with and in proximity to Dilthey.

Indeed, up to now we have spoken of the primordial, a-theoretical domain of lived-experience (a domain that goes untouched by the theoretical-reflective approach) only in anticipation, without showing positively the a-theoretical approach and the a-theoretical lived-experience as such. The pathway, along which the idea of a philosophical primordial science has been exposed up to now, leads to the "methodological crossroads that is decisive for the life and death of philosophy itself,"[55] for the life and death of the anticipated future philosophy. It is the junction of two ways, the theoretical-reflective way and the a-theoretical way. The way of the theoretical-reflective approach to lived-experience is an old and long-established way. But the way of the a-theoretical approach to life and living-experience has so far been drafted only as an idea – and in this respect is not yet an established pathway, but rather one that needs to be blazed. It has not yet been ascertained whether this new trail can even be blazed or travelled. Thus the decision about the life and death of future philosophy projected as idea has not yet been made. Thus the methodological crossroads is an "abyss."[56] The pathway of the exposition of primordial science that has been taken is a way that goes up to this abyss. On this way primordial science falls "into the nothing" and thereby suffers a premature death, namely, the death that occurs when the a-theoretical approach should prove to be blocked. In this case the anticipated primordial science would fall into the nothing "of absolute reification."[57] But that would mean that life and living-experience, the domain of life and lived-experience, would be philosophically thematizable only as a theoretical-reflective objectified object-domain, as is the case up to now. In that kind of decision the projected idea of primordial science would prove to be a mistake for philosophy.

[22] However, the abyss to which the exposition of the idea of primordial science has led is not just an abyss into the nothing, but an abyss that can be leapt over. The decisive question is whether that abyss – that is, the absolute reification of the domain of lived-experience – can be leapt over in such a way that the domain of lived-experience is

---

55 Ibid., 63.
56 Ibid.
57 Ibid.

capable of manifesting in its primordial, a-theoretical condition, prior to its theoretical-reflective objectification. Does philosophy remain bound irrevocably to the singular access to its field of investigation – bound, that is, to the theoretical-reflective approach – or can it successfully "leap to an *other world*"?[58] The "other world" is the world or domain of the a-theoretical. But here, "other world" is not simply another term for the other domain. For "the leap into an *other world*" is, to be clear, a leap "for the first time ever into the world."[59]

To talk of leaping for the first time ever into the "world" is to say that, as long as philosophy is dominated by theoretical and absolute reification [*Sachlichkeit*], it has missed all connection with world *as world*. With the leap into "an other world," an entirely new concept of world emerges. World no longer means the totality of objective beings to be experienced, but rather a whole of what is significant, a significance-whole. World as significance-whole is, however, a phenomenon of world that as such does not manifest itself in the theoretical-reflective approach, but only in the a-theoretical and a-reflective approach. It is the world of living and living-experience, the life-world, but the a-theoretical life-world, which – as we will soon see more precisely – cannot be equated with the pre-scientific life-world of reflective phenomenology.

As we stand at the methodological crossroads, at the abyss, without yet having attempted the leap into the a-theoretical world, and "instead of always *knowing* things [*Sachen*]," we await "*looking-on understanding and understanding looking*."[60] Here for the first time the a-theoretical and a-reflective approach to the primordially scientific field of investigation [23] is designated as a "looking-on understanding" or an "understanding looking" [*zuschauendes Verstehen* or *verstehendes Schauen*]. This is distinguished from theoretical knowing, whose known is only things, what is reified, or what is ob-jectified. For looking-on understanding or understanding looking is also a mode of knowing, but a knowing of a singular kind. Both words in the expression "looking-on understanding" are highly significant. Primordial scientific knowing is above all else an "understanding." But we do not come closer to the sense of this understanding, for example, by remembering Dilthey's distinction between explaining and understanding [*erklären* and

---

58 Ibid.
59 Ibid.
60 Ibid., 65.

verstehen]. For understanding as used in the social sciences itself takes place within the theoretical-reflective attitude. The proper sense of looking-on understanding can only be clarified step by step.

Primordial scientific understanding is one that looks [*schauen*]. But theory and reflection can also be a looking, an ob-jectifying looking. Primordial scientific understanding is not a looking that is ob-jectifying and theoretical, but rather an a-theoretical looking. As such it is a looking-*on* that *stays within the lived-experience that is enacted in living [it]* – and, elevating this into explicitness, it looks-on lived experience. The word *looking-on* [*zuschauen*] is chosen in order to allow the non-reflective and non-objectifying character of understanding looking to become clear. Understanding looking *accompanies* the sense of enactment of living-experience and is thereby capable of interpreting the pre-theoretical essence that is own to lived-experience. The understanding that is non-reflective but that accompanies the looking-on is what is *hermeneutic* in this approach.

Following this first designation of the a-theoretical approach as looking-on in understanding, one can attempt the leap over the abyss. One can try to thematize any lived-experience – which up to now was only a theme of theoretical observation – primordially scientifically in the a-theoretical approach, as indicated. In the lectures from the war emergency semester, the process of investigation does not decide immediately for lived-experience of the surrounding world that is primary in the pre-theoretical domain, but rather, initially, for the specific lived-experience of questioning. The question is: "Is there something?" [24] It will later be shown to what extent this lived-experience is itself not a primary experience but rather is only possible through a modification of the primary lived-experiences of the surrounding world.

The lived-experience of questioning ought not now to be made into an object of epistemological or psychological reflection, in a theoretical attitude. Rather, it should be interpreted in the leap over the abyss in the manner of looking-on in understanding. To look-on, in understanding, the lived-experience of questioning now means: "to comply with the straightforward sense of the question, to understand what lies within it."[61] The "straightforward sense" of the question is what is untouched theoretically – namely, the pure, primordial enactment of this lived-experience. Understanding that which lies *in* this

---

61 Heidegger, *Die Idee der Philosophie* ..., GA 56/57, 65.

lived-experience is possible only if, for this explicit understanding, we do not turn away from the enactment of the lived experience and make the lived-experience into an object of reflection. What is most decisive for this distinction between the reflective and the a-theoretical approach is the difference between (a) going from the living enactment of the lived-experience to take up the lived-experience as something opposite, that is, as object of reflection, and (b) staying within the enactment of the lived-experience such that this enactment is now elevated into explicitness. What lies in the lived-experience of questioning – and needs to be understood – are the "motifs" out of which this questioning draws its life. These motifs are to be understood in such a way that they are "drawn out in listening [*herausgehört*]."[62] Thus, understanding is a looking-on and a drawing-out-in-listening. Hermeneutic understanding is designated as a looking-on as well as a listening.

If in this looking-on and listening attitude of understanding we give ourselves over to the lived-experience of questioning "plainly and simply" – thus without occluding reflection – "we know nothing of a pro-cess [*Vor-gang*], a happening."[63] With the word *pro-cess* one grasps the structure of the lived-experience insofar as this is an object of psychological or conscious-theoretical reflection. In the methodological attitude of looking-on and listening in understanding, I am shown the lived-experience of questioning, but not as a psychic process happening in the soul. [25] The lived-experience of questioning is not shown to me as a psychic event that – over-against as object of reflection – *passes by* me as a reflecting being, and then passes away. Writing the word *process* [*Vor-gang*] with the hyphen is a clue to the objective over-against of the object of reflection. (All things considered, it should be immediately pointed out here that within the theoretical attitude of reflection, lived-experience is manifest in a proper way as an event of the soul and immanent in consciousness. The truth of what psychology and theories of consciousness extract as cognitions about lived-experiences – this truth is in no way in question. The theoretical attitude cannot even be declared false or mistaken. The only issue for hermeneutic understanding is to show that the domain of lived-experience in the non-reflective way of access manifests *other than* in the reflective attitude.)

---

62 Ibid.
63 Ibid.

If the objection is made that lived-experience is obviously a process, in the soul or in consciousness, for understanding looking-on and for listening as well, one would have to counter by saying that, according to this way of speaking of and viewing lived-experience, lived-experience is "already reified."[64] This objection would not be taking lived-experience as such, "as what is there, what shows itself" [als was es sich gibt].[65] With this, the maxim of phenomenological investigation now resounds clearly: "to go back to the 'things themselves.'" This maxim is the first and decisive methodological principle of phenomenology as Husserl expressed it for the first time in his introduction to the second volume of Logical Investigations.[66] The methodological understanding of phenomenology expressed in this maxim is the one that Heidegger made his own. With regard to methodology, primordial science of the a-theoretical domain of lived-experience is meant to be phenomenology – that is, a philosophizing [26] entirely from the things themselves. But in connection with the phenomenological method, "thing" here does not mean the same as in discussions of theoretical-reflective knowledge, which knows things only in the sense of reification and ob-jectification. Thus, we must keep the two meanings of "thing" strictly separate. Things in the sense of phenomenology are phenomena, what show themselves, what call for investigation, insofar as this [i.e., the phenomenon] manifests itself for the investigating gaze precisely as it is composed in itself. When the investigatory gaze is theoretical-reflective from the beginning, then lived-experiences can manifest themselves only as reflected. But within the reflective attitude they manifest as they are in themselves as reflected. The maxim of phenomenological investigation – "going back to the things themselves" – is in and of itself not bound to the reflective approach. Thus the methodological maxim of phenomenology can also guide a philosophizing that is pre-reflective and pre-theoretical.

In terms of the pre-theoretical attitude, the reflective attitude of phenomenology can be characterized as a philosophical attitude that does not allow the phenomenological principle of "going back to the things themselves" to fully unfold. In the hermeneutic understanding,

---

64 Ibid., 66.
65 Ibid.
66 Edmund Husserl, Logische Untersuchungen. Zweiter Band: Untersuchungen zur Phänomenologie und Theorie der Erkenntnis, 6; Huss., XIX/1, 10; ET, I, 252.

lived-experiences show themselves as what they primordially and primarily are only when they can show themselves in their a-theoretical character. Thus, the methodological maxim of phenomenology reaches its full efficacy only in hermeneutic phenomenology. The methodological maxim of "going back to the things themselves" works in its radical sense only when, instead of reflecting on lived-experience and ob-jectifying it, we understand the "pure motifs of the sense of pure lived-experience" from within the full, living enactment of lived-experience – drawing it out in listening, in understanding. The motifs are "pure," and lived-experience is "pure," when they remain pure, that is, free from a reflective objectification.

Before this account of the exemplary lived-experience of questioning approaches any closer an interpretation in (non-reflective) understanding regarding its pure motif, we must say something about the word *Erlebnis/lived-experience*. Indeed, the word-concept *lived-experience* itself "is so worn out and diluted today [27] that it is best to lay it aside."[67] It is worn out because it has been absorbed by the various positions of epistemology and psychology and by theories of consciousness. What chains the various positions together is that they all thematize lived-experience from out of a reflective attitude. The danger is that the worn-out and thereby diluted word *lived-experience* stands in the way of a totally different way of access that is not one of reflection but one of understanding. Thus the primordial scientific enterprise might benefit if it did not hold on to the term "lived-experience" for saying the phenomenon that is to be interpreted in understanding in its undisguised sense of enactment, instead abandoning this word in favour of a word that is not burdened by a theoretical way of observation. If this were so, primordial science could choose to abandon this word for the pre-theoretical domain "if it did not fit so perfectly."[68] But it does fit, albeit only in primordially scientific usage, if we avoid all of the meanings this word has absorbed from the theoretical positions of the psychic and of consciousness and attribute to it only the meaning that is manifest from within the interpretation in understanding of the phenomenon in question. The word *lived-experience* will then be fitting only when it is *heard in a totally new way*. If we simply pay attention to what manifests itself as what is ownmost in the phenomenon in question,

---

67 Heidegger, *Die Idee der Philosophie* ..., GA 56/57, 66.
68 Ibid.

then the word *lived-experience* matches the phenomenal content of the phenomenon in an exemplary way. Then one must even say that "it cannot be avoided"[69] and that no other word could be more precise. But then it is even more a matter of "understanding what its essence is,"[70] which cannot ever be arrived at from any form of psychology and theory of consciousness. But then it is the essence to be revealed in understanding that allows the word *lived-experience* to be heard and understood in a totally new way.

[28] In the effort to interpret in understanding the lived-experience of questioning in "Is there anything at all?", one can initially and tentatively say that I comport myself in it, as something put fully into question. The non-reflective way of access is marked by this challenge: "Let us enact it [the lived-experience of questioning] in full livingness, and let us proceed in accord with this intention and see on the strength of that."[71] Thus, the lived-experience of questioning should not become an over-against of reflection; rather, we should and must remain in lived-experience, must enact it unreflectively and in full livingness – not living in it naively and unexpressly, but from now on expressly. Making explicit what is enacted pre-philosophically and unexpressly makes it possible to engage in the sense of enactment of the lived-experience of questioning and to take notice of this, in order to say what this lived-experience offers for understanding.

For this taking notice, in understanding, of the sense of the living, enacted lived-experience of questioning, however, there appears to be no disconnected I in the sense of the ego from the formula *ego-cogito-cogitatum*. Without the disconnected I, the lived-experience of questioning is a questioning dedication to something with the character of questionability. When we look directly into the living, enacted lived-experience of questioning, there manifests a questioning living-experience of something as questionable, a questioning "living unto something,"[72] without a disconnected I that experiences, without "the sense of referring-back to me."[73] The sense of the lived-experience of questioning has no reference to the disconnected I.

---

69 Ibid.
70 Ibid.
71 Ibid.
72 Ibid., 68.
73 Ibid.

That a disconnected I does not appear cannot mean that the living and living-experience that are to be understood hermeneutically were entirely lacking the I. The sense of the lived-experience of questioning is always somehow in relation to an I, but it is without relation to a disconnected I. The "somehow necessary I-relation and the I" of the lived-experience "cannot be seen in simply observing,"[74] because the questioning I belongs to lived-experience in a way [29] that is other than as a disconnected I. The positing of a disconnected I that belongs to lived-experience is a step taken by psychology and theories of consciousness in order to objectify lived-experience. At the same time, it belongs to the sense of enactment of the lived-experience of questioning that it "is somehow *my* lived-experience."[75] "I am after all there" in the lived-experience of questioning; "I experience it live"[76] – the lived-experience of questioning – in that I enact it in living-experience. The lived-experience of questioning "belongs to *my* life."[77] Yet "it is, in accord with its sense, so very detached from me, so absolutely distant from the I,"[78] because the disconnected I does not belong to it and its sense of enactment. The I in its disconnectedness – as executing I and I-pole – belongs in the way that lived-experience is given in reflection. Within the interpretation in understanding of the lived-experience in its completely alive enactment, how the I belongs to its lived-experiences needs to be marked in another way – not in the way of the disconnected I, but rather in the direction of a mine-ness (*my* life and lived-experience), which belongs constitutively to living and living-experience.

In connection with the question of how I belong to the non-objectified lived-experience, reference will shortly be made to the fact that the non-ob-jectified, pure pre-theoretical lived-experience "is" and that it also has a "now."[79] The "is" refers to the being, the ownmost way of being, of living and living-experience, whereas the "now" indicates the ownmost time and temporality of living and living-experience. The ownmost way in which lived-experience is is the a-theoretical essence of lived-experience that we are seeking to unfold. The ownmost temporality of lived-experience aims at the emerging in time of the

---

74 Ibid., 69.
75 Ibid.
76 Ibid.
77 Ibid.
78 Ibid.
79 Ibid.

lived-experience. This temporality is not the time of the psychic or im-manent consciousness, which belongs to the theoretical and objectified lived-experience, but a temporality that belongs to the full sense of en-actment of a-theoretical lived-experience.

[30] Examining the first results of the interpretation in understanding of the lived-experience that shows itself pre-theoretically, we read: "A plethora of brand new problem-nodes is let loose"[80] – brand new in con-trast to the otherwise only familiar way of observing lived-experiences, namely the theoretical way. "Problems, yes, but on the other hand again something seeable here and there directly, in itself pointing ahead to new sense-connections."[81] Most of what has been shown from the point of view of understanding of the sense of the lived-experience of ques-tioning is a problem that is not yet resolved. But what is "immediately accessible to the look [Schaubares]" has also become manifest, thus yielding the first positive insights into the a-theoretical sense of enact-ment of lived-experiences. For here it was not only a matter of the par-ticular lived-experience, the lived-experience of questioning, but rather that this lived-experience had merely exemplary function.

Having gone a part of the way in interpreting-understanding, we can now achieve "a foundational and essential insight into" the lived-experience of questioning – even if it is a derived and not a primary lived-experience, one that instead turns back to the primary lived-experiences. This insight is directed toward the sought-after essence of the a-theoretical, that is, lived-experience that is not theoretically ob-jectified. From the point of view of theoretical-reflective ob-jectifying, as occurs in psychology and theories of consciousness, the ob-jectified lived-experience has priority and shows itself as a happening that passes by in front of the reflective gaze. In this case, lived-experience as pro-cess or passing-by [Vor-gang] is a happening that has the character of an object.

It is true that lived-experience also has a happening-character from the point of view of interpreting in understanding. But the happening of lived-experience that is untouched by the theoretical is unfathom-ably different from the happening of pro-cess. The lived-experience that manifests itself pre-theoretically is not a pro-cess, but a "happen-ing [Er-eignis]." The ownmost essence and being of the lived-experience

---

80 Ibid.
81 Ibid.

that is not ob-jectified consists in what is now named – in an entirely new way that has yet to be clarified – *a happening*. Living-experience is essentially a happening, [31] because it takes place from within what is own to it, its ownmost [*das Eigenste*]. Living-experience happens [*ereignet* sich] from what is own [*eigen*] to it. Still, with that, this own and ownmost of lived-experience is not yet shown in a sufficiently positive manner. The word *happening* has a primarily indicative character. It indicates and points into the own domain of lived-experience and living, which needs to be interpreted step by step this side of the reflective objectification.

§ 3. Hermeneutic-Phenomenological Disclosing of the Lived-Experience of the Surrounding World

It is true that the hermeneutic attitude in understanding allows the a-theoretical character of lived-experience in general to be brought exemplarily to understanding in looking. However, because the lived-experience of questioning does not belong to the primary lived-experiences of the domain of a-theoretical lived-experiences, the primary and fundamental living-experience of the surrounding world cannot be uncovered by way of itself. Therefore the next and deciding step in the unfolding of the philosophical primordial science of the pre-theoretical domain of living and lived-experience is aimed at the hermeneutic understanding of the lived-experience of the surrounding world.

For this purpose we can "make present"[82] a lived-experience of the surrounding world. Husserl speaks of bringing to mind the

---

82 [Translator's note: The German word here is *vergegenwärtigen*. The word is used by both Husserl and Heidegger, as this paragraph will show. The word is used in German as "make present" or "visualize." Its roots are in the word *Gegenwart*, which means "the present." *Gegenwärtigen* means "to make present." For Husserl *vergegenwärtigen* is a kind of *terminus technicus*: "making present" takes place temporally in intentional analysis. (Cairns suggests the word *presentiate* to translate this Husserlian term.)

For Heidegger it means "letting what presences [emerging, *Anwesendes*] come to meet us [*begegnen*] in a making-present [*Gegenwärtigen*]." Cf. *Sein und Zeit*, 326. With this in mind, we could translate Husserl's word *vergegenwärtigen* here as "representing in the mind," that is, in intentional analysis. On the other hand we could translate Heidegger's word *vergegenwärtigen* as "a letting-come-to us of what presences/emerges, in a making-present." All of this is implied in this paragraph from von Herrmann.]

lived-experience in consciousness that is to be thematized phenomenologically in each case. "Making present" belongs to the procedure
of phenomenology. For phenomenological analysis we do not need an
actually present enacted lived-experience; rather, we can at any time
bring such to presence. But for Husserl the phenomenological making-
present takes place within reflective ob-jectification. In contrast to that,
for Heidegger the making-present takes place in hermeneutic understanding. The hermeneutic making-present remains – in contrast to [32]
reflective making-present – within the living enactment of the lived-
experience. The lived-experience of the surrounding world that is to be
brought to presence non-reflectively, but hermeneutically, stands "in a
certain contrast"[83] to the lived-experience of questioning, insofar as the
latter is itself not a primary lived-experience of the surrounding world,
but rather arises out of this through modification.

We bring a familiar lived-experience of the surrounding world "to
givenness"[84] before us. Here, too, with this word Heidegger is referring back to Husserl's phenomenological language usage. For Husserl,
to make-present a lived-experience for the purposes of a phenomenological thematizing also means "to bring" this "to givenness." Later
in the lectures from the war emergency semester of 1919, Heidegger
will exclude this phrase from the language usage of hermeneutic phenomenology, because in terms of what it says, it belongs in reflective
phenomenology. Immediately in connection with this he reaches for a
third language marker, to show how we should turn in understanding to the lived-experience of the surrounding world. We should "enter
into" the lived-experience of the surrounding world. This word hits
the mark best to say the intention of the hermeneutic understanding
of the lived-experience of the surrounding world. In contrast to the
theoretical-reflective thematizing, in which we bring the living enactment of lived-experience to a standstill and make the lived-experience
into an object of a new lived-experience of reflecting – instead of this,
for the hermeneutic understanding we stay with the living, enacted
lived-experience and through the modification of expressing we bring
ourselves into the site of interpreting the lived-experience of the surrounding world in accordance with its sense of enactment.

---

83 Ibid., 70.
84 Ibid.

That lived-experience of the surrounding world into which we should now place ourselves, in order to interpret it in understanding as expressly enacted according to its sense, stems from the natural and daily situation of living and lived-experience in the university. The students enter the auditorium, go to their seats, and from there look at the lectern, whence they will be spoken to. But the instructor too goes into the auditorium and steps behind the lectern, in order to speak to the students from there. Now, the exemplary lived-experience of the surrounding world is supposed to be the common view of the lectern. Seeing the lectern [33] is a lived-experience of the surrounding world, because it is seeing this thing in the surrounding world, the surrounding world of the auditorium. With that is also said that, in seeing the lectern, not only do we see it, but also and at the same time and along with it we see that which surrounds the lectern.

The most decisive question now is: What do we see when we look at the lectern, whether as those who are spoken to from the lectern or as those who speak from the lectern? A most decisive answer belongs to this most decisive question. For it decides whether we remain in the theoretical-reflective attitude and thus do not make the leap over the abyss, or whether this leap into the primary and fundamental realm of the a-theoretical world-life and the a-theoretical life-world succeeds.

The first answer to the question asked could be: We see brown surfaces that intersect at right angles. Another answer would be: We see a somewhat large box, the bottom part of the lectern, and a smaller box set on it. Both of these answers vouch for an attitude that slides a consideration between what is seen and the seeing – a consideration that is meant to determine what is actually seen. This consideration that is interposed prevents us from simply naming what we have primarily always already seen before we deliberate about it. Such an interpolation of considerations has the character of observing and reflecting from a distance, in which we have truly already leapt over the always already seen and understood. The interposed consideration is the *theoretical*, which, in the thematic determination of what is seen in the surrounding world, is posited prior to what is seen a-theoretically, thus obstructing this a-theoretical. With these examples of answers to the question about what is truly seen, one sees that the theoretical does not mean this or that scientific theory. The theoretical that obstructs the hermeneutic-understanding access to the lived-experience of the surrounding world and what is lived in the surrounding world – this theoretical is not initially even theories, but rather a reflecting observation that as such has already closed itself off from any access to the hermeneutic [34] understanding of what is primarily lived and seen.

After we find inappropriate the first and second answers to the question of what we actually see when we see the lectern in the auditorium, where we listen or speak, there follows a third answer, one that says what we truly see, but this time in an appropriate manner. Seemingly, the answer does not say anything: we see the lectern in common, even if with this difference – for the students one speaks of the lectern as seen, whereas the instructor speaks from the seen lectern. As much as this answer may appear to say nothing, it is still decisive, because it steers those who give the answer away from the considerations they have employed and back to what the seen shows them. The seen lectern does not have to be explained by means of reflection as this or that. Rather, hermeneutic understanding is meant to expressly go along with the sense of enactment of seeing-the-lectern and to see the lectern as it shows itself, for and in the seeing. As we enter the auditorium, the lectern shows itself to our seeing of the surrounding world in its own meaning, in its *significance*, by which it belongs to the surrounding world of the auditorium. The unmediated, primary, and fundamental – as that which the seen lectern shows itself in seeing – is itself significant *as this*, in this or that way. A further task of hermeneutic understanding would be to bring the significance of what is significant closer to interpretation. We do not see the lectern primarily in these or those perceptible properties, to which then is added the meaning "lectern." We see the lectern primarily as in the surrounding world, as significant in this or that way. Only when we retain this primary finding of hermeneutic understanding of the lived-experience of the surrounding world do we gain the first foothold into the primary a-theoretical domain of lived-experience.

In "pure lived-experience," which is kept free of the reflective way of access, there lies no "founding-connection, as if I would first see brown, intersecting surfaces that then reveal themselves to me as box, then as desk, and then as lectern, [35] as if I had, as it were, stuck what makes it a lectern onto the box, like a label."[85] Calling for a *founding-connection* belongs fundamentally to the theoretical attitude and dominance of the theoretical interpretation of what is primarily an a-theoretical living- and lived-experience. Husserl's reflective phenomenology is directed

---

85 Ibid., 71.

precisely by the basic thought of the founding-connection. Husserl calls for a founding-connection for seeing the thing in the surrounding world as well as for the thing seen in the surrounding world. According to the guiding thought of founding-connection, knowledge of the surrounding world is fundamentally sense experience, and above all sense perception. Accordingly, the thing in the surrounding world is fundamentally and at its core a sensory, perceptual thing. Other intentional lived-experiences are grounded in this pure sense perception, and we grasp in these intentions the primary and merely perceived thing in these or those meanings. Seen in this way, the lived-experience of the lectern is a whole from out of a grounding and a grounded lived-experience. Correlatively, the seen lectern is a grounding thing in perception, in which is grounded the meaning "lectern" that is apprehended. Here the meaning of the lectern, what is significant to it, is something grounded, secondary and not primary. The lectern-ness of the lectern resembles a label that is stuck onto the primary, material perceptual thing.

Regarding this guiding thought of a connection to a fundament, it is said: "The whole thing is interpretation that is off the mark and misconstrued, turning away from purely looking-into the lived-experience."[86] The epistemological and epistemologically phenomenological interpretation of the lived-experience of the surrounding world as a connection to a fundament is "off the mark" because it is "misled" – misled by a guiding thought that stems from a theoretical consideration and that is not drawn from the lived-experience of the surrounding world itself. The theorizing fore-grasping [Vorgriff] of the connection to a fundament turns away "from purely looking-into the lived-experience."[87] "Looking-into" is a [36] further designation of hermeneutic understanding through which the already named looking and listening are elucidated. For hermeneutic understanding we can only look into the lived-experience if we abide in it and its living enactment and do not step out of the enactment of the lived-experience in order to make it an object of reflecting lived-experience. In understanding looking at seeing the lectern, what manifests itself to us is not something grounded, a thing of perception, which then is grasped as a lectern. When in understanding looking we do not let ourselves be waylaid by an intervening

---

86 Ibid.
87 Ibid.

theoretical consideration, the only thing that shows itself is what is significant in its significance, in this way or that. If hermeneutic understanding strictly follows the phenomenological maxim "to the things themselves," then it has to adhere only to what shows itself to that understanding, without any mediating theory. Adhering to this phenomenal finding, however, applies to all further steps of interpreting in understanding the lived-experience of the surrounding world.

Because it is with the thought of connection to a fundament – which guides Husserl's reflective phenomenology – that the ways of hermeneutic and reflective phenomenology part, it would be well to first pay closer attention to Husserl's position.

(a) Lived-Experience of the Surrounding World in the Theoretical-Reflective Attitude (Husserl)

At the beginning of "Considerations Fundamental to Phenomenology" in *Ideas I*, § 27, "The World of the Natural Attitude: I and My Surrounding World,"[88] Husserl offers an initial phenomenological description of the living-experience of the surrounding world, one that is still held in the natural, pre-transcendental attitude. I am conscious of a world, my world, which is spread out endlessly in space and [37] becoming as well as having become endless in time. My consciousness of my surrounding world says "above all, I find it immediately in intuition, I experience it."[89] Following this description, the intuitiveness in which my surrounding world is given to me in the manner peculiar to consciousness is one of sense experience. This is immediately explained according to its various ways: "Through seeing, touching, hearing, etc., in the various ways of sense perception, corporeal things are *simply there for me*, in some kind of spatial distribution."[90] Already here it becomes clear that the primary access to the surrounding world, which supports everything else, is the ways of sense perception. Accordingly, the surrounding world that is given to consciousness is primarily and at its core a world experienced by the senses, a perceptual world, and the things in the surrounding world are primarily things and perceptual things of sense experience.

---

88 Husserl, *Ideen zu einer reinen Phänomenolgie und phänomenologischen Philosophie. Erstes Buch: Allgemeine Einführung in die reine Phänomenologie*, 48ff.; Huss., III, 57ff.
89 Ibid., 48; Huss., III, 57.
90 Ibid.

Yet the surrounding world that is mine and that I am conscious of is "not there as simply *a world of mere things* [*Sachenwelt*], but rather in the same immediacy as *world of objects with value, world of goods, a practical world.*"[91] What Husserl calls "world of mere things" is the pure world of experience or perception and therefore of what in things is accessible through sense perception as perceivable, material bodies. Husserl does not want to say that we are first conscious of merely perceptual things and then *afterwards* are conscious of additional other aspects and meanings. Rather, we are conscious of the things of the surrounding world *simultaneously* as things with specific value- and practical-characteristics. "I see at once the things configured in front of me, as with reified properties as well as with value-characteristics such as beautiful and ugly or agreeable and disagreeable or pleasant and unpleasant."[92] Furthermore, the things of the surrounding world are immediately there "as things for use," the "table" with its "books," the "drinking glass," the "vase," the "piano."[93] In conclusion, this phenomenological description says: "These value- and practical-characteristics [38] also belong *constitutively to the ob-jects on hand as such.*"[94]

The value- and usage-characteristics of things in the surrounding world are grounded in the sensorily perceivable reified properties. The things of the surrounding world are known as spatially extended and formed bodies, coloured in this way or that, hard or elastic – and, based on that, given the meaning of table or drinking glass, given the aesthetic characteristics of beautiful or ugly and, in the affective realm, of pleasant or unpleasant. Here the fundament-thinking is manifest. Indeed, one is conscious of the things of the surrounding world at one and the same time in their merely reified properties and in their usage- and value-characteristics. But both the consciousness of the surrounding world and the things of the surrounding world of which one is conscious are in their constitution a whole of grounding and grounded. What does the grounding are the modes of consciousness of sense perception, in which sensorily perceivable bodies become objective. Those other acts of consciousness are grounded in these grounding modes of consciousness, in which the sensorily perceived material body is apprehended in its practical and aesthetic-affective characteristics. The

---

91 Ibid., 50; *Huss.*, III, 59.
92 Ibid. [Translator's note: Cairns says "merely material determinations."]
93 Ibid.
94 Ibid.

sensorily perceivable layer of what is material-corporeal supports the apprehending layer of the practical-aesthetic-affective characteristics, in which the experienced world of bodies – which is at bottom sensory – is apprehended.

(b) Lived-Experience of the Surrounding World in the A-Theoretical Attitude (Heidegger)

The ways of hermeneutic and of reflective phenomenology part at this fore-grasping of the guiding thought of a founding-connection. For the thought that is "founding" is not drawn out from the lived-experience of the surrounding world; rather, it is brought to the lived-experience through a theoretical consideration. The thought of a founding stems from the theoretical way of accessing the lived-experience of the surrounding world. [39] As long as this guiding thought is determinative in its fore-grasping, the way to the a-theoretical essence of the lived-experience of the surrounding world is closed off. For Husserl the surrounding world is at bottom a world of sense experience and, based on that, a usage- and values-world. The practical characteristics of the things for use are grounded in their sensorily experiential reified aspects. Broadly speaking, the usage-character in this way of seeing resembles a label that is attached to the thing presented in sense perception.

Over against this way of interpretation, hermeneutic phenomenology says: "I see the lectern, as it were, all at once."[95] This sentence does not intend to say the same as reflective phenomenology stresses, namely, that we do not see the thing in the surrounding world first as a perceived thing and then as a thing for usage, but rather that we see it as "table" all at once – which, however, as the "seen" is a gathering together from the grounding reified properties and a grounded usage-character. Seeing the lectern "all at once" emphasizes the hermeneutic way of seeing – that we see the lectern as significant in this way or that – *without* its significance being something grounded by a grounding. What is significant for hermeneutic understanding of the lived-experience is that which we encounter immediately – without mediation through a perceivable corporeal layer.

But does that mean that for hermeneutic understanding seeing the lectern is only a seeing of what is significant, without a sensory

95 Heidegger, *Die Idee der Philosophie* ..., GA 56/57, 71.

seeing? Does hermeneutic understanding ignore the sense perception? Absolutely not! But sense perception loses its independence- and
founding-character. For interpretation in understanding, it is manifest
that sense experience *is embedded* in the understanding of the significance of the lived-experience of the surrounding world. What is primary and guiding in the lived-experiences of the surrounding world
is the understanding of significance of the significant things in the surrounding world. The guiding understanding of significance shows [40]
to sense experience the *how* of perceiving that accompanies the lived-
experiences of the surrounding world. Sensory perceiving is included
in the living understanding of significance. And because it is included,
it is not independent and grounding; thus, in the lived-experiences of
the surrounding world, we do not perceive primarily and at bottom a
material corporeal layer, which is apprehended in practical meanings
through grounded intention of consciousness.

The lectern that I see all at once, as significant in this or that way, I see
"not only isolated" but also "as positioned too high for me."[96] I would
see the lectern as isolated if I were to see it outside my interaction with
it in using it. But I see it as significant in this or that way in its significance from within my interactive understanding. For the significance
of what is significant has a connection to my interaction with what is
significant, which in turn is guided in its enactment by the understanding of significance. "Positioned too high for me" says that my interaction in usage with the lectern, which is significant in this or that way, is
hindered. All that belongs to seeing the lectern is determined from out
of the understanding of the significance of this thing in the surrounding
world. The sensory seeing of the lectern remains totally sheltered in the
understanding of significance.

But I also see the lectern "in an orientation, a lighting, a background."[97] Orientation and lighting are also determined from out of the
understanding of significance. I stand behind the lectern in such a way,
and the lectern is at the same time lit in such a way, that I can be undis-
turbed as I speak to the students from it. The background of the lectern
is its situation in the surrounding world. It is in the middle of other
things in the surrounding world, which for their part are significant

---

96 Ibid.
97 Ibid.

in this or that way. The significance of the lectern is not self-enclosed or isolated. Rather, it points to the significances of the things standing around, points to the whole of the significance – that by which I understand the surrounding world of the auditorium.

One could object to this conclusion of interpretation in understanding of seeing-the-lectern, by saying that only those [41] who are familiar with this significance and with the whole of significance of the auditorium and the academic world – only they understand this thing in the surrounding world as a lectern. And that, when catching sight of the lectern, the others apparently see merely a material corporeal thing without its specific meaning. This would then prove that the thing of the surrounding world that is seen is still at bottom a mere body with this or that apprehended meaning. Such a person, one who is not familiar with the academic world because s/he has perhaps never entered an auditorium, could be, for example, "a peasant from high in the Black Forest."[98] If the more specific significance of a lectern is unknown to them, what do they see? Perhaps that it is "place for the teacher."[99] Thus they also see the lectern as a significant place in this or that way, and not as a mere body. Even if they were to see the lectern only as a box or as an assemblage of boards, they would not see a naked body, but something significant with the character of a box or an assemblage of boards, for storing this or that.

The lack of familiarity with the whole of significance would be worsened, and the significance that belongs to this whole would be strengthened, if we were to think of "a Senegalese" who is "suddenly" transplanted "from his hut"[100] into the auditorium. Whereas the peasant had something of an understanding of the academic attitude and thus saw the lectern as a place for the teacher, the Senegalese appears to perceive a merely material thing. But if he, from his perspective, were to see that which we see as a lectern as something "having to do with magic"[101] or as something "behind which one would find good protection against arrows and thrown stones,"[102] then, although he would not see the lectern from within its significance, he would see it from within another significance that is familiar to him. But that would mean that

---

98 Ibid.
99 Ibid.
100 Ibid.
101 Ibid., 72.
102 Ibid.

he would not see the lectern unfamiliar to him as a pure perceptual thing [42], but rather as something significant. However, were it to happen that he did not see the lectern from within a whole of significance that is familiar to him – but rather encountered the lectern as something with which "he cannot do anything"[103] – then he would understand this also as not simply a perceptible thing outside any horizon of significance. Rather, he would encounter the lectern in its "unfamiliarity as a tool."[104]

"Unfamiliarity as a tool" says that, to the Senegalese on his seeing the lectern, its significance is kept hidden. Unfamiliarity as a tool is not negation of any significance at all, but rather privation. The Senegalese's seeing-the-lectern is composed in such a way that the significance of what is seen cannot be understood from the horizon of significance. His seeing is not a naked perceiving, but one that is aimed at understanding what he encounters as significant in this or that way. Thus Heidegger can say: "What belongs to the meaning of 'unfamiliarity as a tool' and what belongs to the meaning of 'lectern' are absolutely identical as regards their essential core."[105] The example of the Senegalese is meant to demonstrate hermeneutically that this specific human being and this human group understand something immediately as meaningful in this or that way, while the others perceive naked corporeal things, because they are unfamiliar with a horizon of significance. This example should lead to the insight that the human as human lives essentially from within the horizons of significance, that these horizons are what is primary and immediate in his living in the surrounding world, and that in his lived-experiences he essentially lives in what is significant. Given that it belongs to the essential constitution of human life to live and to experience from within the horizons of meaning, we essentially never encounter merely things of sense experience, but rather always only meaningful things. Their significance is what lets them be things of the surrounding world. For surrounding world does not mean the whole of things of sense experience – does not at all mean a whole of things or objects – but rather a whole of [43] significances, from out of which we encounter things as significant, as things of the surrounding world.

---

103 Ibid.
104 Ibid.
105 Ibid.

The hermeneutic analysis of lived-experience of the surrounding world reaches its first decisive result: "In the lived-experience of the lectern there comes *to me* something from an immediately surrounding world."[106] This is the world of significance, which is not mediated through a world of perception. What belongs to the surrounding character of the surrounding world of significance are not sensorily perceived objects, which are apprehended in this or that meaning; rather, "the significant is what is primary."[107] The surrounding character as what is significant comes to me "immediately, without any detour in thought about seizing or grasping things."[108]

But that means: "Since I live in a surrounding world, its meaning to me everywhere and always is that everything is worldly."[109] "Its meaning to me" means that I encounter what is surrounding [me] in the world, it speaks to me in its significance. Its meaning to me is "everywhere," not only here and there – otherwise I would also encounter mere things of perception – but rather essentially everywhere. Its meaning to me is "always," not only every now and then – otherwise I would occasionally encounter mere things of experience – but rather essentially always. Everything that I encounter as surrounding [me] is "worldly," that is, significant from out of the world of the whole of significance, from out of the world of significance.

Everything that I encounter in a surrounding world signifies to me, addresses me in its meaning, in its significance. Everything that signifies to me is worldly, meets me in its significance from out of the worldly whole of significance. Everything that concerns me in its worldly significance, "worlds."[110] The verbal form *to world* is not a neologism of Heidegger's. We witness the word "to world" in older texts, and there it means: to lead an excellent life, to live well. Heidegger draws on the common word in our older language, in order to mark its happening-character, [44] in which the surrounding things concern us, address us, *meet* us. All things of the surrounding world "world," because they concern me from out of the world of significance in their worldly significance, as significant in this or that way.

---

106 Ibid.
107 Ibid., 73.
108 Ibid.
109 Ibid.
110 Ibid.

§ 4. Lived-Experience as Happening or as What Passes By

On the basis of the hermeneutic-phenomenological analysis of the lived-experience of the surrounding world that we have just performed, we can now go more in depth into the question of the *structure* of lived-experience. This was already indicated as happening [*Ereignis*], in contrast to what-passes-by [*Vor-gang*], which is the structure of theoretically objectified lived-experiences.

In order to take up again the hermeneutic understanding of lived-experience of the surrounding world, we must bring it to mind in such a way that we expressly transport ourselves into it. When Heidegger occasionally speaks of "looking into my seeing relation to the lectern given in the surrounding world," this phrasing is inappropriate for hermeneutic understanding, because it revives the thought of an ob-jectifying thematizing. If the sense of seeing-the-lectern is kept cleanly from theoretical ob-jectifying, then what shows itself to me is not a disconnected I as the I-pole of my lived-experiences (in the same way that a disconnected I did not show itself in the previous discussion of the lived-experience of questioning). In the lived-experience of the surrounding world of seeing-the-lectern, I live-into the lectern as understood in its significance. In this living-into of mine, "something lies before me,"[111] but not me as an I-pole. In my experience of living-into, "*my* I proceeds fully from out of itself and resonates *along with* this 'seeing.'"[112] Resonating along with this living-experience of seeing is the way in which my I belongs to my living-experience. This own I experiences what is surrounding, and this worlds for it only in the way that the I resonates along with the living-experience of the surrounding world. [45] Wherever and whenever it worlds for me, wherever and whenever I encounter what is significant, "*I* am somehow totally with it."[113]

In the lived-experience of the question "Is there anything at all?," "I do not encounter myself"[114] in the manner of my resonating along with the living-experience. But this "anything at all" from the lived-experience of questioning also does "not world."[115] For when we grasp

---

111 Ibid.
112 Ibid.
113 Ibid.
114 Ibid.
115 Ibid.

every possible aspect of the surrounding world as anything at all, as in this lived-experience of questioning, then the aspect of world and of what is significant is "snuffed out."[116] Along with this erasing of the aspect of world, my own I as what resonates along with the lived-experience of the surrounding world is repressed. In determining any-thing at all as object, the "oscillating, this co-emergence of what is mine is stifled."[117] Being an ob-ject as such "does not touch *me*";[118] my I does not resonate along with the determining cognition. The I that deter-mines in cognition "is no longer the I"[119] that resonates along with the living-experience of the surrounding world. If the living-experience is a determining of what is experienced, then it is "now only a rudi-ment of living-experience; it is an abandoning of living [*Ent-leben*].[120] "Abandoning of living" is not some neologism of Heidegger's, but was used in the seventeenth century in the sense of "to kill" (*vita privare*). In the living-experience of determining cognition, living-experience is deprived of its primary, originary character of living-experience, the living-experiences of the surrounding world. What is cognized in the cognitive living-experience is "removed"[121] from the proper nearness that it has in the living-experience of the surrounding world, "lifted out of the actual [primary] living-experience"[122] of the surrounding world.

A happening in the surrounding world, significant in this or that way as experienced in that world, can – like every significant something – be ob-jectified and perceived as an objective happening. The ob-jectified [46] happening can be described as "pro-cess," because now it no lon-ger comes across as significant, but instead it passes by the knowing I. For the knowing I the ob-jectified happening of the pro-cess has "only the relation of being-cognized, this deflated I-relationship, reduced to a minimum of living-experience."[123] Ob-jectified things and connec-tions with things show themselves only in cognizing, in the theoretical comportment for the "theoretical I."[124] In theoretical comportment, I in

---

116 Ibid.
117 Ibid.
118 Ibid.
119 Ibid.
120 Ibid., 73f.
121 Ibid., 74.
122 Ibid.
123 Ibid.
124 Ibid.

my knowing am "aimed at"[125] something. Being theoretically aimed at something, I do not live as an "historical I" that moves to the worldly. The I that resonates in the lived-experiences of the surrounding world is the historical [*das historische, das geschichtliche*[126]] I in contrast with the theoretical I. The historical I lives into the lived happening of the surrounding world as something worldly. In cognizing, the theoretical I stands over against an ob-jectified happening, which can be called pro-cess, because it [the ob-jectified happening] passes-by the theoretical I, without addressing and identifying the theoretical I as something worldly.

With that we now stand before a *second* notion of "pro-cess [*Vorgang*]." Pro-cess as passing-by was first designated as the character of reflective and ob-jectified lived-experiences, because these too pass by the reflecting I. But just now the word pro-cess [as what passes by] [*Vor-gang*] named the happening of the surrounding world that is ob-jectified in the knowing living-experience and that loses its primary character of significance in this ob-jectification. We must differentiate these two notions of "pro-cess," even if they have in common the fact that pro-cess as passing-by is in each case what is known in theoretical cognition.

The second notion of "pro-cess" was introduced into the course of the war emergency semester as a name for an ob-jectified happening, because here a worldly happening of the surrounding world as theoretically known by a cognizing living-experience is contrasted with the pre-theoretical lived happening of a living-experience of the surrounding world. By means of this contrasting of a theoretical knowing and a pre-theoretical [47] living-experience of the surrounding world, the essential structure of the primary lived-experience of the surrounding world and – insofar as the theoretical lived-experience is a modification of the pre-theoretical lived-experience – also of the derived theoretical lived-experience is determined.

Both mutually contrasted lived-experiences have one and the same lived character, one that is on the one hand *known theoretically* and on

---

125 Ibid.
126 [Translator's note: Later on in the book, von Herrmann will make the distinction between *geschichtlich* and *historisch*. At that point I will translate the two words differently, as "historical" and "historiographical" respectively. But here he does not make this distinction thematic, even putting the two words side by side without distinguishing them. Thus here I translate both words as "historical."]

the other hand *lived pre-theoretically*. Take the phenomenon of the sunrise: on the one hand it is an ob-ject of astronomy's knowledge, while on the other hand it is what is worldly as a living-experience of the surrounding world. That now the theoretical-knowing living-experience of the astronomer is not to be understood theoretically and reflectively, but rather hermeneutically, follows already from the fact that we are prompted to "transpose"[127] ourselves into the theoretical comportment of the astronomer. Following the sense of carrying out the theoretical living-experience, we understand how the phenomenon of the sunrise, stripped of its primary significance in the surrounding world, reveals itself to the theoretical I as a mere happening of nature, which passes before it.

The same phenomenon of the sunrise can be experienced in a pre-theoretical way of lived-experience, in which it comes across to the one experiencing it as worldly and significant. It is important here to note that Heidegger does not choose the rising of the sun that is experienced by each one of us, but rather chooses a *distinctive* living-experience of the sunrise – distinctive because it is a lived-experience of the surrounding world that is poetized [*gedichtetes*] in a great poem. It is the shared lived-experience of the chorus of the oldest Theban from the *Antigone* by Sophocles. On the first morning after the victorious defensive battle, seeing the sunrise, the chorus speaks:

> Ray of the sun!
> fairest morning brilliance ever
> risen over the seven-gated Thebes,
> at last you shine forth,
> O eyes of golden day,
> and light up the city,
> strolling over the streams of Dirce.[128]

It is the hermeneutic insight that poetizing moves in the pre-theoretical domain of the living-experience of the surrounding world – but, in comparison with [48] the living-experience of the surrounding world that is outside the poetic domain, in a distinctive manner. For it is poetizing

---

127 Ibid.

128 [Translator's note: The English version of this text is from *Antigone* (Clayton: Prestwick House, 2005), ll. 100–5. The translation has been slightly modified.]

that opens up the possibilities of the living-experience of the surrounding world and that makes it experiencible [*erfahrbar*]. Hermeneutic-phenomenological thinking, too, sees its primary field of investigation in the domain of the pre-theoretical living-experience of the surrounding world. The task that is own to it is to unveil the structural content of the living-experience of the surrounding world, to understand it hermeneutically. Because hermeneutic-phenomenological thinking shares with poetizing *the same field* of the primary living-experience of the surrounding world – poetizing reveals in a distinctive manner the possibilities of the living-experience of the surrounding world, while thinking interprets the lived-experiences of the surrounding world in their pre-theoretical structure-content – thinking can, as in our case, turn to a poetizing, in the manner of a dialogue, in order for poetizing to give thinking directives for its penetration of the living-experience of the surrounding world. In other words, hermeneutic-phenomenological thinking is understood from the very beginning as a nearness to poetizing, even as both remain separated by a subtle but clear difference.

The challenge of "understanding both lived-experiences, then again, according to their own sense"[129] refers to the two lived-experiences of the surrounding world (seeing the lectern and looking at the sunrise). To understand these according to their own sense means to understand them hermeneutically in their sense of enactment. The question now is whether, in this going along hermeneutically with the sense of enactment of the living-experience of the surrounding world, we "comprehend" these lived-experiences of the surrounding world "as pro-cesses," that is, "as ob-jects that are presented and determined."[130] This would be the case if we reflectively make the lived-experiences of the surrounding world into objects, ob-jects of a reflecting act. In the objectifying reflection, the lived-experience of the surrounding world unfurls like an object for the reflecting act; it proceeds like a passing-by. When the reflecting act reflects on the lived-experience [49] of the surrounding world, it is outside the lived-experience of the surrounding world. In contrast to that, when hermeneutic understanding engages in the sense of enactment of the lived-experience of the surrounding world, it stays within the lived-experience of the surrounding world that is being interpreted. But with that the lived-experience of the surrounding world

---

129 Heidegger, *Die Idee der Philosophie* ..., GA 56/57, 75.
130 Ibid.

cannot become object of reflection, cannot be ob-jectified in a present-ing. Hermeneutic understanding takes place as looking-into the sense of enactment of the living-experience, which is possible only because it stays in the lived-experience of the surrounding world. The answer to the question whether in hermeneutic understanding we comprehend the lived-experience of the surrounding world as what-passes-by is a clear No.

But does establishing that the hermeneutically understood lived-experience of the surrounding world has no pro-cess or passing-by character – does this deny any character of happening for the lived-experience of the surrounding world? In seeing the lectern, "something does happen"; "I am there with my full I"; "it is a lived-experience specifically for me."[131] That is the designation in hermeneutic seeing of seeing-the-lectern, and the lived-experience thus seen hermeneu-tically is a happening. But it is not the happening of something that passes by that is reflectively presented, but rather a happening of lived-experience with which I go along when I see it hermeneutically. This ownmost character of happening, which is own to it and is not a reflec-tively objectified lived-experience, is not a passing-by [*Vor-gang*] but a *happening* [*Ereignis*]. This word is a term that determines the essential structure of the lived-experience, above all the primary lived-experience of the surrounding world. Therefore *Ereignis* here does not name that which, otherwise in our language, we name an event, a somewhat sa-lient occurrence. We have yet to clarify what *Ereignis* as a conceptual structure says. Prior to clarifying, it must immediately be stressed that a "remainder of *Ereignis*" is present in the lived-experience of question-ing. For the lived-experience of questioning is not a primary but rather a derived lived-experience. It is only the primary and fundamental lived-experiences that show the full, unabbreviated character of *Ereig-nis*, whereas the lived-experience of questioning that is derivative of the lived-experience of the surrounding world shows a reduced character of *Ereignis*.

[50] In the hermeneutic engagement with the happening of enact-ment of the lived-experience of the surrounding world, the living-experiencing does not pass by me [*mir vorbeigehen*] (pro-cess [*Vor-gang*]) as the reflected lived-experience; "rather I myself make it own [*er-eigne*]

---

131 Ibid.

to me" – that is, the lived-experience "is owned according to its essence"[132] [*er-eignet sich seinem Wesen nach*]. The essential character of lived-experience can be marked in two ways: I experience in that I make the lived-experience own to me, or the lived-experience is owned. As essence of lived-experience, *Er-eignis* means: I make the lived-experience own for myself, the living-experience is owned. When I look into the lived-experience hermeneutically, I do not understand it as an ob-jectified pro-cess, but "rather as something entirely new."[133] With a view to what is *own* [*das Eigene*] to lived-experience, that which is entirely new takes the name *Er-eignis*. It is something entirely new because the *Er-eignis* character of lived-experience has never been experienced as the essence of lived-experiences. For up until now lived-experience and living-experience were only the theme of a reflecting ob-jectifying, which closes off the *Er-eignis* character of lived-experience. The a-theoretical, hermeneutic understanding is an entirely new means of access to lived-experiences, in which these show themselves for the first time in their *Ereignis* character, which is otherwise kept hidden. When I look "straightforwardly," that is, without reflective objectification, but not without methodological way of access – understanding hermeneutically – I see "nothing psychic,"[134] because psychic being is a reflectively ob-jectified lived-experience, which as such keeps itself locked up with regard to its *Ereignis* character.

Now, what does the word *Er-eignis* say more precisely? What meaning does the word element *-eignis* have? One might think that *er-eignen* means *an-eignen*. I make the living-experience own to me would then mean: I acquire the lived-experiences from somewhere or other, in order to live from the lived-experiences acquired like that. My acquired, own lived-experiences would then be my property [*Eigentum* in the usual meaning]. But it is this meaning of *-eignis/own* as property that is rejected.

Lived-experiences are in their essence *Er-eignisse*, insofar as they "live from within the own and life lives only thusly."[135] The word element [51] *–eignis*/own points thus to the own [*das Eigene*] and not

---

132 Ibid.
133 Ibid.
134 Ibid.
135 Ibid.

to property. Insofar as lived-experience lives from within its own, it is as lived-experience *Er-eignis*, according to its essence. In *Er-eignis*, the word element *-eigen* names what is own to living-experience and to living; the prefix *er-* from *Er-eignis* is the same as the prefix *er-* from lived-experience [*Er-lebnis*]. *Er-*, ur-, as prefix means: originary, primordial.[136] *Because it lives from within the own, originary living as living-experience is Er-eignis.* Understood and interpreted hermeneutically, lived-experiences are *Er-eignisse* because they live from within the own of living and living-experience. The pre-theoretical concept of *Er-eignis* that is gained hermeneutically is determined, not from "property/*Eigentum*," but rather from "own/*das Eigene.*" I enact my lived-experiences, my respective living-experience, from what is own to living and living-experience. What is own to lived-experience of the surrounding world is its essence, its ownmost essence, and thus what Heidegger later will call the existence [*Existenz*] of Dasein. In this way "*Ereignis*" is also not a hermeneutic concept that demonstrates exhaustively the own and ownmost of living and living-experience. Rather, the concept "*Er-eignis*" points only to what is own in living and living-experience, which has still to be revealed. The task of philosophical primordial science is a hermeneutic-phenomenological analytic of what is own to pre-theoretical living and living-experience. Such an analytic of living and living-experience in its *Er-eignis* essence is the first and decisive step of a hermeneutic-phenomenological analytic of Dasein.

This elucidation of *Er-eignis* as essence of living and living-experience also shows clearly that this early concept of *Er-eignis* must be strictly differentiated from the later being-historical concept of *Ereignis*. In *Er-eignis* [the word used in 1919], as essence of living and living-experience, *-eignis* has the meaning of own and ownmost; whereas, in *Er-eignis* [the word used from the 1930s onward] as the belonging-together of enowning throw [to Dasein] and Da-sein's enowned throwing-open, *-eignis*/own says as much as "ownhood [*Eigentum*]." For from the enowning as enowning throw, the being of humans – as the enowned throwing-open – becomes, *as en-owned*, the ownhood of the enowning truth of being. Therefore, it is a coarse misinterpretation to fancy that Heidegger's being-historical concept of enowning (from the 1930s) [52] is tied to his early hermeneutic of living in its *Ereignis* character.

---

136 [Translator's note: I have translated the *ur-* as "primordial."]

§ 5. Obsession with the Theoretical as Hindrance for Insight into the Domain of Living-Experience of the Surrounding World

It is true that in the previous sections what was inherent in the a-theoretically articulated lived-experience of the surrounding world – even in its essential structure, the *Ereignis* character – was drawn into the hermeneutic field of vision. But such a hermeneutic-phenomenological insight can only be counted as secured if it holds its own against every epistemological objection. One of the many objections of this kind that could be held against this primordially scientific analysis is that it has flounced around in suppositions and assumptions, instead of considering "what is immediately and primarily given."[137] Epistemology, too, invokes what is immediately, primarily given. That almost sounds like the call of the phenomenologist: "Go back to the things themselves!" But what is the immediately and primarily given for the epistemology that is expressed here, and what is the immediately and primarily given for hermeneutic phenomenology?

Epistemology can make the point that what is truly immediate and primary in my lived-experience of the surrounding world are sensations and sense data. For, this argument goes, we can set aside everything that belongs to the lectern in view, "strike off everything up to the mere sensation of brown and [...] make this itself into an object," so that this shows itself as "primarily given."[138] The sensation of brown is something primarily given, because it is the first and foundational thing in lived-experience that cannot be stricken off. It is an immediately given, because I do not need to reveal it mediately, as I do in the case of its external cause. [53] The sensation is not mediately, but immediately there. It appears thus to be *the* aspect of the lived-experience of the surrounding world from which one is to proceed in secured fashion, for the epistemological explanation of what is lived in this lived-experience.

How must hermeneutic phenomenology handle this objection and this point about the primarily and immediately given of the sense data? Epistemology could point to what for it is truly immediate and primary only by way of theory (observation) and reflection (reasoning). But for hermeneutic phenomenology that approach hides and makes invisible

---

137 Ibid., 85.
138 Ibid.

what is actually immediate and primary. For the sake of what it wants to understand, it avoids the way of access of the destructive resolution and instead transposes itself expressly into the lived-experience of the surrounding world. In this hermeneutic attitude, what is untouched, immediate, and primary is the lectern, which comes across in lived-experience as what is significant in this way or that, from within the whole of significance. Hermeneutically, I see the lectern as what is significant. In my living-experience I live into what is significant. Neither in my naive living-experience nor in my hermeneutic understanding of this living-experience do I see "sensations and sense-data; I have no consciousness at all of sensations."[139] Husserl's reflective phenomenology already stresses that in our lived-experiences of perception we are not relating to sensations; rather, on the basis of the purely subjective sensations of brown in the perception, we are relating intentionally to the objective brown of the lectern. In connection with Husserl, Heidegger also says: When I see the brown colour, I do not see it "as sensation of brown, as a moment in my psychic processes."[140] But in characterizing how I see the brown colour, hermeneutic phenomenology is differentiated from reflective phenomenology. For Husserl the brown colour that is seen is a material aspect of the primary, grounding perceptual thing; for Heidegger I see the brown colour "in an integrative meaning-connection with the [54] lectern."[141] Here what is primary and immediate is the lectern as significant. I do not see the brown colour as a thing-character over against its use-character; rather, I see the brown-being of the lectern from within its character of significance. In the elaborations gone over just now, there is on the one hand the critique carried out in common with Husserl, namely of non-phenomenological epistemology; on the other hand there is Heidegger's additional critique of Husserl's reflective-phenomenological characterization of perceptual sense-qualities.

The insistence by epistemology that I can strike off from my lived-experience of the surrounding world everything except the sensations, such that these sensations are revealed as what is outstanding, in the sense that they cannot be stricken off – this insistence is not denied as a possibility. But the question remains: For whom are these solely

---

139 Ibid.
140 Ibid.
141 Ibid.

reflectively gained sensations immediately given? Obviously only for the one reflecting, and not for the one experiencing them. For as the experiencer, I do not experience the "datum 'brown' as a moment of sensation in the same way as I experience the lectern."[142] In the brown that is apprehended as datum there is no longer any worlding. Only that which worlds, that which one encounters from within the worldly significance-connection, is what is actually immediate and primary and is not touched by a consideration that is interposed. When I apprehend brown as datum of sensation, "my historical I"[143] no longer resonates with this apprehension. Rather it has withdrawn in favour of the theoretical I.

The self-givenness of the sensation is not immediate, but mediated through abstracting reflection. The "sensation is perhaps present, but only by my destroying the worldly aspect, by my striking off, setting aside, deactivating my historical I, and doing theory, primarily *in* the theoretical attitude."[144] The theoretical attitude, which supposes that it can recognize the lived-experience of the surrounding world as such by way of abstracting reflection, [55] destroys the living-experience of the surrounding world and the surrounding world that is experienced. Both the sensation of brown and the simple brown colour make up the primary and immediate, for the non-phenomenological epistemology and for reflective phenomenology, only insofar as they are already doing theory and keep within the theoretical attitude, "which in turn and according to its sense is possible only as destroying the lived-experience of the surrounding world."[145]

An a-theoretical understanding of space and time belongs constitutively also to the a-theoretical lived-experiences of the surrounding world. What the war emergency lecture course indicates concerning this is basically the anticipation of what will later in *Being and Time* be set forth as the spatiality of Dasein (§§ 22–4) and as the concern with time (world-time) (§ 79). A spatial understanding of the surrounding world is expressed in the question "Where is the closest way to the cathedral?"[146] The spatial orientation expressed here cannot be grasped

---

142 Ibid.
143 Ibid.
144 Ibid.
145 Ibid.
146 Ibid., 86.

by the scientific-geometric understanding of space. But we would also not go far enough if we approached this natural understanding of space from the perspective of reflective-phenomenological analysis of perception. The a-theoretical understanding of space is rather determined from within the worldly understanding of significance. Therein lies the difference between the hermeneutic-phenomenological and the reflective-phenomenological understanding of space within the life-world. In the question about the closest way to the cathedral, we are not asking about the quantitative length of the spatial distance. The nearness and distance in the understanding of space of the surrounding world that appear here do not have a quantitative character, but rather a significance-character.

The same is true for the understanding of time of the surrounding world: it does not have the sense of the physically measurable time and not at all a primarily quantitatively conceivable time. The spans of time to which I am related in my lived-experiences of the surrounding world are determined from within my relationships in the surrounding world to what is significant in the surrounding world.

All "sense phenomena of lived-experiences of the surrounding world,"[147] to which the understanding of space and time of the surrounding world then also belong, [56] cannot be clarified philosophically if "I destroy their essential character, abolish them in their sense, and project a theory."[148] The essential character of sense phenomena is the a-theoretical character that is own to them, their en-owning character, which all sense phenomena of lived-experiences of the surrounding world share. An epistemological "explanation" of lived-experiences of the surrounding world via abstracting reflection and a return to structural elements such as sensations is "fragmentation," and that means "destruction"[149] of lived-experiences of the surrounding world in the character that is own to them. Philosophical penetration of a-theoretical lived-experiences of the surrounding world is not possible via explanation, but rather only through interpretation in understanding, which, by going along with the sense of enactment of lived-experiences, reveals their sense phenomena without destroying them or making them transparent. Epistemological efforts that go back to sensations, in order

---

147 Ibid.
148 Ibid.
149 Ibid.

to comprehend from these the lived-experience of the surrounding world and the surrounding world that is experienced therein, want to "explain something that one no longer has as such or can or will let prevail as it is, as such."[150] From the very beginning such epistemological explanations no longer have the lived-experiences as such in their purview and are not able to let them be as the lived-experiences of the surrounding world that they are for hermeneutic understanding. The own character of a-theoretical lived-experiences has already been covered over by the epistemological approach. For every approach that explains lived-experiences of the surrounding world and its surrounding world theoretically, the whole of the a-theoretical domain of lived-experience crumbles away. Theoretical explanations of lived-experiences of the surrounding world and the surrounding world itself cannot reach this domain at all, once they have already enclosed themselves in the theoretical approach to the question.

In the face of this situation, which goes with every epistemological approach, it must be said: "It is not only naturalism, as one has fancied (Husserl, Logos article), it is [57] the general dominance of the *theoretical* that deforms the genuine problematic."[151] The genuine problematic is that of an unobstructing and non-distorting interpretation of lived-experiences of the surrounding world and the domain of the lived-experience generally. Husserl rightly saw an obstructing way of access to lived-experiences of consciousness in the naturalizing that happens under the guidance of natural science, as is shown above all in experimental psychology. In his famous essay "Philosophy as Rigourous Science" (1910–11) he develops his phenomenological critique of naturalism. But releasing lived-experiences from their psychological naturalization did not yet gain the "genuine problematic" of the domain of lived-experience. For, from the very beginning and as a matter of course, Husserl's phenomenological critique kept within a reflective-theoretical attitude, in which the pure essence, the *eidos*, of lived-experiences and their ideal lawfulness were to be extracted. To gain the genuine problematic of lived-experiences, it is not sufficient simply to reject the naturalistic approach. The genuine problematic is secured for hermeneutic phenomenology only if every theoretical-reflective way of access is abandoned. Not only naturalism's domination over the domain of

---

150 Ibid.
151 Ibid., 87.

lived-experience, but also the general dominance of the theoretical – which determines Husserl's reflective phenomenology as well – deforms the genuine, that is, a-theoretical problematic.

The general dominance of the theoretical means the absolute "primacy of the theoretical"[152] in philosophy. It belongs to this general dominance that philosophy and with it the philosophical turn to the domain of lived-experience do not initially find themselves on the untouched foundation of the a-theoretical, in order then to abandon this a-theoretical by means of a first step into the realm of the theoretical. "One is already from the beginning and always in the theoretical,"[153] because the actual a-theoretical is at this time not [58] even seen as such, insofar as the a-theoretical always already stands in theoretical pre-grasping. "One takes [the theoretical] as self-evident, especially when one wants to do science and even more epistemology [theory of knowledge, *Erkenntnis-theorie*]."[154] Again and again the apparently telling argument is that *scientific* philosophy has to be philosophical *theory*. As long as one understands "theory" only in the meaning of philosophical reflection, which makes explicit and thematically penetrates what is inexplicit and unthematic in pre-philosophical enactment of living, equating scientific philosophy and theory would apply. But as soon as we question more closely the way of access and proceeding of philosophical theory, we see that theory as such is observation from a distance, ob-jectifying explanation, and objectifying reflection. But theory in this narrow and strict sense proves to be a way of access to the domain of lived-experience that closes off this domain in its most characteristic, that is, a-theoretical way of enactment, so that, whereas the domain of lived-experience shows itself, it does this only in the theoretically modified fashion, which no longer allows one to discern anything of its a-theoretical character. In contrast to that, hermeneutic phenomenology is indeed scientific philosophy, but not theoretical. Instead it is an a-theoretical science that is capable of making philosophically visible the a-theoretical domain of lived-experience as such.

But here again we have to stress that the theoretical as such is not to be thrown out. Rather, after the primacy of the a-theoretical is comprehended, we now ask the genuine question about the origin of the

---

152 Ibid.
153 Ibid.
154 Ibid.

theoretical from out of the a-theoretical; we ask about the "essence and sensory genesis of the theoretical," as well as the possible "performance"[155] of the theoretical.

Up until now we have considered two lived-experiences of the surrounding world – seeing-the-lectern and looking at the sunrise – which we have rudimentarily interpreted hermeneutically in their undistorted, a-theoretical essence. But both lived-experiences had exemplary character. For they were [59] meant to let us see "that we often, and indeed most of the time, live in the surrounding world."[156] We experience in the context of the surrounding world not only "often" but "most of the time." In *Being and Time* it says that we live "initially and most of the time"[157] in the surrounding world. For the "living-experience of the surrounding world is not random."[158] Initially and also most of the time we always live a-theoretically in a surrounding world. For the a-theoretical surrounding world is nothing random, appearing every now and then. Rather, the a-theoretical living-experience of the surrounding world forms the "reigning realm"[159] of human living-experience. But the "profoundly tenacious attachment to the theoretical is certainly still a massive hindrance for truly getting an overview of the reigning realm of living-experience of the surrounding world."[160] The a-theoretical living-experience of the surrounding world is the essential composition of human living. In contrast to this, we are geared to the theoretical "only by exception."[161] Indeed, the possibility of a theoretical frame of mind is part of human life. However, although we live a-theoretically in the surrounding world as long as we live and experience, we do not necessarily have to live theoretically as well. We can eschew the theoretical experience, but not the a-theoretical living-experience of the surrounding world. That shows what it means that experiencing the surrounding world makes up the reigning realm. The fact that the living-experience of the surrounding world is the reigning realm of human life means that our experience is "initially and most of the time" of the surrounding world, that is, everyday-natural. But the "profoundly

---

155 Ibid.
156 Ibid., 88.
157 Heidegger, *Sein und Zeit*, GA 2, 58; EA, 43.
158 Heidegger, *Die Idee der Philosophie …*, GA 56/57, 88.
159 Ibid.
160 Ibid.
161 Ibid.

tenacious attachment [of philosophy] to the theoretical"[162] in the sense of general dominance and primacy of the theoretical in traditional philosophy constitutes [60] a hindrance that is difficult to overcome in "truly getting an overview"[163] of the reigning realm of living-experience of the surrounding world. We truly comprehend this only when we hermeneutically understand and interpret, without obstruction, the a-theoretical domain of the living-experience of the surrounding world in its breadth, depth, and complexity. The lived-experience of feeling also belongs to the lived-experience of the surrounding world. We determine this theoretically – that is, with the help of a pre-formed psychological theory or a theory of the science of consciousness – when we construe it either as a merely subjective feeling state or as an intentional experience that is founded in another intentional lived-experience. In contrast to that, we only grasp its a-theoretical character when we follow the sense of enactment of the lived-experience of the surrounding world hermeneutically, and see how the living-experience of the whole of significance of the surrounding world and the respectively experienced encountering of the significant are determined from within the holistic feeling, from a holistic attunement that regulates the living-experience of the surrounding world. Within the hermeneutic perspective, feeling, the attunement, is not grounded in a sense experience, but rather belongs to the primary way of encountering the surrounding world and what belongs to the surrounding world. In the unobstructed a-theoretical feeling, I am experiencing the surrounding world primarily in nearness to the surrounding world that is experienced in feeling and to what is significant that is experienced in feeling.

Because they belong to the reigning realm of the living-experience of the surrounding world, the lived-experience of the lectern and the lived-experience of the sunrise are not lived-experiences that are contrived or "dragged in by the hair,"[164] not artificially constructed. Now we must ask whether the surrounding world, when it is experienced, is "given"[165] for the one experiencing it. At the same time we must ask whether the experienced surrounding world is "given" as what is significant for the one who understands hermeneutically. In answering

---

162 Ibid.
163 Ibid.
164 Ibid.
165 Ibid.

this question, the challenge is again to live-into the livingness of a lived-experience of the surrounding world. In the lived-experience of the surrounding world, is the surrounding world "given" to me? Is "givenness" the accurate designation for how I [61] experience the surrounding world in each case? This question is of particular significance for our project of allowing Heidegger's and Husserl's concepts of phenomenology to emerge in their contrast. For it is Husserl who, in his reflective phenomenology, speaks of the immediate and corporeal "givenness" of the perceptual thing for the perceiving experience. By contrast, for hermeneutic settling into the aliveness of the experience of the surrounding world, the experienced surrounding world is not "given" but rather "presents itself to" the experiencing one in its significance.

So how do we not experience the surrounding world as a given? The surrounding world as a given is no longer what is encountered a-theoretically, but rather is something that is handled theoretically. The surrounding world that is designated as given is "already pushed away from me, the historical I."[166] The experiencer who experiences a given is no longer the I who experiences the surrounding world in time – and in this sense a historical I, that is, one living historically – but rather the incipient theoretical I. If we designate the surrounding world as a given, then the worlding of the surrounding world is "no longer primary." "Given" is already a quiet, inconspicuous, but indeed truly theoretical reflection"[167] on the surrounding world. For Husserl this reflection means that the surrounding world is grasped and given primarily as perceptual thing. Husserl's designation of the perceptual givenness of the surrounding world comes from out of the presupposed theory that the surrounding world must be made objective primarily in sensory lived-experiences.

"Givenness" is a "theoretical form" distinct from "the way of encountering" that designates the a-theoretical self-showing of what is significant as surrounding world when we experience and deal with it. The idea that "givenness" actually means the essence of the immediately surrounding world in its character as surrounding world – this idea is "fundamentally wrong."[168] This verdict is directed against

---

166 Ibid.
167 Ibid., 88f.
168 Ibid., 89.

Husserl's reflective phenomenology of lived-experiences of the surrounding world. For Husserl the surrounding world is [62] at bottom foundational as perceptual world, and the surrounding world is immediately *given* and *grasped* as perceptual thing in the perceiving ways of presenting. Calling for givenness of the surrounding world as the way in which this is experienced in the manner peculiar to consciousness results from the fundamentally theoretical positing that the surrounding world in its manifold meaning-characteristics is at bottom a perceptual world that is presented with its perceivable thing-qualities. For Husserl and reflective phenomenology the character of the surrounding world is encountered in this givenness in experience of the surrounding world. But for Heidegger and hermeneutic phenomenology that approach amounts to an "inverted" philosophical opinion, inverted in the literal sense, for it claims that the derived theoretical givenness is immediate and primary and thereby keeps locked up the actual immediate and primary, the essentially a-theoretical composition of the surrounding world.

The phenomenological view that givenness gets to the essence of the immediately surrounding world in its character as surrounding world carries "only one good thing, that it brings to a head the unjustified predominance of the theoretical precisely within the essentially a-theoretical domain – bringing it to the clearest expression thinkable – precisely by putting what is fundamentally and essentially foreign to theory back into a theoretical form, thus 'lifting' the surrounding world 'up' into the theoretical."[169] The unjustified predominance of the theoretical in traditional philosophy is brought to a head by reflective phenomenology when from the very beginning it examines the "essentially a-theoretical domain," "that which is fundamentally and essentially foreign to theory,"[170] within the theoretical-reflective attitude, whereby the a-theoretical character of the domain of lived-experience is closed off, to such an extent that it remains totally invisible for phenomenological analysis. In the method by which the surrounding world and the lived-experiences of the surrounding world are already specified for the designation of the natural-prephilosophical attitude of the experiencer [63] – namely, as the world of sense experience given in a manner peculiar to consciousness or as the world of significance that presents itself to

---

169 Ibid.
170 Ibid.

us – reflective and hermeneutic phenomenology differ radically from each other. Reflective phenomenology establishes itself in the theoretical attitude, but grounds this in the a-theoretical that it has discovered. Hermeneutic phenomenology arises as possibility from within the primordial experience of the a-theoretical domain of living and lived-experience. Its urgent concern is to interpret the a-theoretical domain in its purity.

Theorizing the pre-theoretical can take place in phases. A first step consists in positing the surrounding world as "given," especially in the way that "givenness" means "the first objectifying scanning of the surrounding world," which is, however initially only a first representing of the surrounding world "before the *still* historical I,"[171] so that here the I is still historical self-temporalizing I and not yet the theoretical I. A second step of making-theoretical happens when "the genuine sense of the surrounding world, its meaning-character, is, at it were, excavated."[172] The first step may occur when the reflective-phenomenological view, arising from the pre-theoretical enactment of living, turns to the surrounding world as the whole of the significant and sets this up as merely "given" prior to reflective interpretation. The second step occurs with reflection on the living-experience of the surrounding world and what is intentionally experienced therein, in that already at the outset of this reflection the meaning-character of the surrounding world is set up as grounded in the perceptual layer of things in the surrounding world. By means of this step of reflection the significance-character of the surrounding world is lifted out of its quality of being immediate and primary. But with that the significant surrounding world that was brought forth in the first step of theorizing only as "given" becomes a merely sensorily experiencible thing-world, in which the whole of significance of the surrounding world is merely grounded. The surrounding world of what is at bottom merely perceptual things "still has [64] qualities, colour, hardness, spatiality, extension, weight,"[173] that is, the perceivable thing-characteristics that make up the supporting basis for the practical world, the world of commodities and the world of values. The originarily, that is, the a-theoretically lived space of the surrounding world [*Umweltraum*] has now become a mere "room for

---

171 Ibid.
172 Ibid.
173 Ibid.

things"[174] [*Dingraum*]; in the same way, the originarily a-theoretical and become-timely time of the surrounding world has become a mere "time for things."[175] The making-theoretical can thus happen as "process of the continuing and destructive theoretical infection of the surrounding world."[176]

For sure, the word *thing* cannot in every case be referred back to the theoretical attitude. In the enactment of living of the a-theoretical attitude of living-experience of the surrounding world and with respect to what is experienced, we can ask: "But what sort of thing is *that*?"[177] What is meant here is not a thing to be known theoretically, but rather something of the surrounding world whose character as surrounding world, that is, whose significance, is still hidden from the questioner. The question is put from the pre-theoretical attitude of living and living-experience.

The thing-character of the mere thing makes up an "original domain,"[178] which, however, is not the primary one that founds everything else. Rather it is "distilled from out of"[179] what is primary and foundational of the surrounding world's totality of significance. In the domain of "mere things," "worlding" is "obliterated."[180] "Worlding" is the term for encountering the surrounding world in its significance-character that belongs to a whole of significance, to the world. The mere thing in its categorically identifiable and interpretable thing-character is designated as what is real in its "reality."[181] The "real" here means what is actual, existing, in its actuality, its existence in the external world. [65] In the meaning of existence as well as the whatness, reality is a theoretical characterization of what is experienced, which itself, however, is only possible on the basis of the a-theoretical encountering of the surrounding world in its primary significance. The fact that world in its worldly character is the foundation or source for the thing in its reality is dealt with in *Being and Time* in a fundamental way in § 43, "Dasein, Worldhood, and Reality."

---

174 Ibid.
175 Ibid.
176 Ibid.
177 Ibid.
178 Ibid.
179 Ibid.
180 Ibid.
181 Ibid.

In the transition from the pre-theoretical comportment of life into the theoretical attitude, what is significant in the surrounding world is "de-signified," such that what shows itself is now only the being-real of the thingly surrounding world. Correlatively, the a-theoretical living-experience of the surrounding world is stripped of ever knowing the real as such. Also part of this process of de-signifying and stripping of life is the fact that the a-theoretical I that shows itself in time, the histori-cal I, is "de-historicized."[182] Now, the theoretical I is that of theoretical knowing of real things. The making-theoretical of the pre-theoretical life and living experience of the surrounding world takes place as de-signifying, stripping of life, de-historicizing [*Ent-deutung, Ent-lebung, Ent-geschichtlichung*].

For reflective phenomenology the sense experience of the thing – the sensory experiencing of perceptual things in their perceivable thing-qualities – is what founds the pre-scientific knowledge of the world. Seen from the hermeneutic-phenomenological primordial science, the experience of the thing that is set out in this fashion is indeed also lived-experience – not an a-theoretical one, but rather a lived-experience that is handled theoretically. Insofar as this lived-experience has its origin in the a-theoretical lived-experience of the surrounding world – and this the most alive lived-experience – as a thing-experience this lived-experience is "stripped of life,"[183] that is, it becomes lived-experience without life. In this way the living-experience shows "levels of living-ness."[184] The primary level of highest livingness is the pre-theoretical experience of the surrounding world, from out of which a series of lev-els can arise, each with increasing theorizing and thus decreasing liv-ingness. [66] Therefore, stripping-of-life does not mean withdrawal of living-experience generally, but rather the withdrawal of the livingness of the living-experience.

Whenever the making-theoretical is made absolute, its "origin from within 'life'"[185] is not seen. But the theoretical is also made absolute in that place where a distinction is made between the pre-scientific and the scientific, as happens in reflective phenomenology. For the pre-scientific is not seen in its a-theoretical character. Rather, it is handled

---

182 Ibid.
183 Ibid., 90.
184 Ibid.
185 Ibid., 91.

and thematized in a theorizing-reflective way of access – an approach by which the truly a-theoretical life and the a-theoretical life of the surrounding world withdraw into phenomenological invisibility.

The process of increasing ob-jectifying is a process of stripping-of-life, the decline of livingness of the living-experience. Heidegger calls the crossing point from the a-theoretical living-experience of the surrounding world in its full livingness to the first level of ob-jectifying: one of the most difficult problems. The question is: Where does one cross the border between the a-theoretical enactment of life and a first ob-jectifying representing of what is experienced? Because reflective phenomenology, in accord with its own approach, reflectively objectifies life and living-experience as life of consciousness, it is not an interpretation of the fully living experience of the surrounding world. In actual fact, reflective phenomenology keeps to the foundation of the de-signified surrounding world, the living-experience that is stripped of life, and the de-historicized I. It is on this foundation, which is given direction by the reflective-theoretical approach, that reflective phenomenology looks for its theoretical evidence of the experienced surrounding world, of the ways of lived-experience, and of the experiencing I.

As phenomenology, hermeneutic phenomenology, too, looks for the evidence of its phenomena. But the a-theoretical surrounding world (and correlatively the a-theoretical ways of living-experience of the surrounding world) "has its genuine self-showing in itself."[186] The worlding way of encountering the surrounding world "is not theoretically established, but rather is experienced 'as worlding.'"[187] [67] And what is experienced as worlding is not brought phenomenologically to theoretical evidence, but rather to a-theoretical self-showing. A-theoretical self-showing says that within hermeneutic interpretation what is a-theoretically experienced, along with the a-theoretical living-experience, is not handled and modified theoretically, but rather is preserved as a-theoretical. The effort [to preserve] genuine self-showing of the a-theoretical living-experience and its "experienced" is the primordially scientific methodological task of hermeneutic phenomenology – a task that is the exact opposite of a way of proceeding that is naive and detached from science. The phenomenological effort for self-showing

---

186 Ibid.
187 Ibid., 94

of the a-theoretical life and the a-theoretical life-world eventually finds its fruition in the hermeneutic phenomenology of Dasein in *Being and Time*.

§ 6. The How of Phenomenological Disclosure of the Domain of Lived-Experience

Now that, in covering the way just gone, we have elaborated what is fundamental to the thematic field of investigation of primordial science and its hermeneutic way of disclosure, we can turn mindfully and in a more intensifying way to the phenomenological problem of methodology.

It is "the problem of methodological capture of lived-experiences generally, i.e., the question: How is a science of lived-experiences as such possible?"[188] Thus, this is a question of the *how* of the methodological capture, of the way of philosophical science. The emphases focus on the method, the science, and their how. Given that the capture of lived-experiences is to be a methodological one, this capture is science. But it is science in a wholly new sense: not theoretical science, but a-theoretical science. Here it becomes clear that the [68] a-theoretical does not exclude either method or science. In actual fact the a-theoretical is the signal for an essentially new sense of method and science. At the same time, however, the method in the new sense remains phenomenology. But the new sense of method also takes hold of phenomenology and leads to its transformation. It is the transformation of reflective phenomenology into hermeneutic phenomenology. For Husserl, phenomenology is reflective disclosure of the domain of lived-experience; for Heidegger, it is hermeneutic disclosure of the domain of lived-experience. Now we have to investigate and determine more clearly the way of proceeding of reflection on the one hand and hermeneutics on the other.

The concern is to clarify "the main feature of the methodological position."[189] It is the methodological position of hermeneutic phenomenology over against that of reflective phenomenology. But at the same time Heidegger stresses that the previous and current reflection that is to be enacted still stays "on the preliminary stage of phenomenological

---

188 Ibid., 94.
189 Ibid.

method."[190] As he does later in *Being and Time*,[191] he distinguishes here a "preliminary stage," a "pre-grasping," of phenomenology, from a full-blown concept of phenomenological method or from the "idea of phenomenology." This can be given only after the primordial science of the a-theoretical domain of lived-experience has been wholly or to a large extent carried out. As the *outline* of the new draft of the third division of the first part of *Being and Time* advises, the "idea of phenomenology" was planned for the third part of the lecture-series published in *The Basic Problems of Phenomenology.*[192]

Before Heidegger turns to a critical countering of the descriptive-reflective way of disclosing lived-experiences, he offers a summary designation of the hermeneutic disclosure of the lived-experience of the surrounding world and of the [69] lived-experience of the mere thing. Here resounds the methodological challenge: "We should thus enact the lived-experience of the surrounding world in full livingness,"[193] which for hermeneutic understanding is not, as it were, a stepping out of life in the lived-experience of the surrounding world, but rather a living in full livingness *in* the lived-experience of the surrounding world. But in order to be able to come to a hermeneutic understanding of this lived-experience, we must at the same time look to this lived-experience in which we live. At another place Heidegger spoke, not of looking to [*auf*] but of looking-into and listening-into [*hinein*]. The "into" fits better the sense of hermeneutic understanding than the "to," which can be easily misunderstood in the sense of reflecting being-directed-to. It is only in hermeneutic looking-to as looking-into the lived-experience of the surrounding world that we can study this for what it is. But now it is not only a matter of achieving the hermeneutic looking-to, in order to be able to say in interpretation which sense-moments make up the lived-experience of the surrounding world. Now it is more a matter of a methodological designation of hermeneutic seeing and understanding. Therefore we are challenged to look into the hermeneutic looking-to, in order to study "the *how* of the first looking that was enacted."[194] In that we look to the lived-experience that is enacted in full living, we can

190 Ibid.
191 Heidegger, *Sein und Zeit*, GA 2, 46; EA, 34.
192 Heidegger, *Die Grundprobleme der Phänomenologie*, GA 24, 32.
193 Heidegger, *Die Idee der Philosophie ...*, GA 56/57, 98.
194 Ibid.

interpret this hermeneutically (not reflectively). But when we look to the hermeneutic looking-to, we can characterize the how that is own to this hermeneutic looking into the lived-experience of the surrounding world. Characterizing this how of looking-to means determining the hermeneutic seeing in the character that is own to it and marking it off from reflective seeing.

Heidegger emphasizes that the "absoluteness" of seeing [...] is not to be gained in one fell swoop, for example with an artifice and knack, but rather initially only in such fashion that we eliminate all relativities (which are essentially theoretical preconceptions)."[195] [70] The "absoluteness of seeing" here means the detaching of hermeneutic seeing from all preconceptions that are of theoretical origin and that as such hinder the a-theoretical-hermeneutic seeing. Even Husserl stresses that the capacity for phenomenological seeing is "not easy to acquire,"[196] although he means the *reflective* seeing of phenomenology. Both reflective-phenomenological as well as hermeneutic-phenomenological seeing require practice.

Now, when it further says, "We looked at and into the lived-experience of the surrounding world,"[197] we have to distinguish this [hermeneutic] looking-to from that [reflective] methodological looking at the looking-to. In the hermeneutic looking into the lived-experience of the surrounding world – for example, seeing-the-lectern – what emerges is that in this lived-experience of the surrounding world there is no "positing of the thing [*Sachsetzung*]" and no "consciousness of givenness."[198] A positing of the thing in the lived-experience of the surrounding world takes place whenever this is seen as an underlying perceptual experience in which we are intentionally related to the perceptual thing with its thing-qualities that are perceivable by the senses. In its basic stratum as world of perceivable bodies, the surrounding world is "given" in and for consciousness. Positing of the thing and consciousness of givenness manifest themselves only where the corporeality as the sustaining fundamental stratum and sense perception as primordial experience are applied. But reflective phenomenology is determined by means of this approach.

---

195 Ibid.
196 Husserl, *Logische Untersuchungen*, II/1, 11; Huss., XIX/1, 16; ET, I, 256.
197 Heidegger, *Die Idee der Philosophie* ..., GA 56/57, 98.
198 Ibid.

In hermeneutic looking-into the lived-experience of the surrounding world no "ob-jectifying"[199] is manifest, to the same extent that there is no positing of the thing and consciousness of givenness. Seeing-the-lectern is not an ob-jectifying act, in which the lectern is given as object in such a way that it exists and is present. Consciousness of existence and of being-present does not belong to the sense of [71] a seeing-the-lectern that is hermeneutically understood. The reason is that seeing-the-lectern is not primarily a sensory perceiving of a thing given as a body, but rather the seeing understanding of what is significant in its belonging to the whole of significance. The surrounding world, instead of being given as something present, "wafts away"[200] in the experiencing comportment. In that it wafts away, it carries in itself "the rhythm of lived-experience."[201] In the lived-experience of the surrounding world, the surrounding world is experienced not as present and given but rather "as this rhythmic" aspect of lived experience. The wafting away of the surrounding world and its rhythmic aspect belong to that which we already have designated as encountering, in contrast to being-given. The surrounding world and its character as surrounding world are not grasped in ob-jectifying; rather, they are encountered in accord with the respective rhythms of the experiencing comportment.

In delimiting the lived-experience of the surrounding world, "a lived-experience of a mere thing" has already been interpreted hermeneutically several times. The hermeneutic interpretation of a lived-experience of a mere thing is not the same as a reflective interpretation of such a lived-experience. The mere-thing experience – the mere perception of a body, for example – is itself possible only as a basic modification of the primary lived-experience of the surrounding world. For hermeneutic understanding of the lived-experience of the thing, "a remarkable break between the experiencing and the experienced"[202] emerges. The experience of the perceptual thing has "completely broken out of the rhythm of the even minimal character of living-experience."[203] In the lived-experience of the surrounding world, experiencing and the experienced form a unifying onefold, which is outlined by means of the respective rhythms of the experiencing comportment. In the lived-experience of

---

199 Ibid.
200 Ibid.
201 Ibid.
202 Ibid.
203 Ibid.

the mere thing, this onefold is broken into two, because the merely perceiving living-experience, as a living-experience stripped of life, shows another rhythm, to which belongs the breaking up of experiencing and experienced. This world of mere sense-experience [*Erfahrungswelt*] and the thing-experience [*Erfahrungsding*], as they are experienced, [72] are no longer affected by the living rhythm of the living-experience of the surrounding world. The experienced thing of perception "stands" there "for itself."[204] It does not present itself, as does the surrounding world, for an experiencing interaction; rather, it is only "meant in cognizing."[205] In contrast to the experienced – that is, not ob-jectified – surrounding world, the "ob-ject domain" is "only meant," in such a way that "cognizing *targets* it."[206] The "being-meant of everything thingly is the sense of reality"[207] over against the significant surrounding world, which is not "meant" in the living-experience of the surrounding world – [the sense of reality] not being that which the living-experience "targets."

When Heidegger here speaks of "meaning" and "targeting" of cognition and of things as "meant," he has in mind the intentionality of cognizing experiencing. But that does not mean that he comprehends intentionality only as an essential characteristic of theoretical cognizing. He wants to point out that, when Husserl designates the essence of intentionality of living-experience as a meaning and targeting, he knows intentionality only in its theoretical form. But intentionality is not only a theoretical phenomenon, as it shows its primary form in the a-theoretical lived-experiences. Thus intentionality belongs to the essence of the pre-theoretical domain of lived-experience. It is only from this origin that the lived-experiences that are handled theoretically and the purely theoretical lived-experiences show the essential character of intentionality. But if intentionality belongs primarily to the realm of the pre-theoretical, then it does not allow itself to be characterized in this field as a meaning-of and targeting. The experiencing interaction with the lectern also does not experience this as a thing meant, but rather as something significant within the comporting interaction with it. The significant is not meant; rather, it is encountered from within its significance for the significance-understanding interaction. The a-theoretical

---

204 Ibid.
205 Ibid.
206 Ibid.
207 Ibid.

intentionality is at play within this interaction and the correlative encountering of it, whereby it is interacted with in understanding.

[73] Because Heidegger, for his hermeneutic countering of the descriptive reflection of Husserl's phenomenology, quotes several core sentences from sections of *Ideas I* that are pertinent for the thematic of phenomenological reflection, it is appropriate that we ourselves now turn to these passages from Husserl.

(a) Husserl's Method of Descriptive Reflection

Descriptive reflection is a method not only of transcendental phenomenology, but also of the pre-transcendental phenomenology of the *Logical Investigations*. In section 3 of the Introduction in volume II of the *Logical Investigations*, "The Difficulties of Pure Phenomenological Analysis,"[208] Husserl basically deals with descriptive reflection as the method for access to psychic experiences.

Phenomenological analysis is accomplished in an "unnatural direction of intuition and thinking."[209] In the *natural* attitude of lived-experience we are wrapped up "in *enactment* [*Vollzug*] of the manifold acts coming one after the other"[210] and *naively* posit the objects that are meant in the sense of these acts as existing, in order to determine them as so posited. In the phenomenological attitude we are to go *against* the *natural* way of enactment of lived-experiences, pull ourselves back from the natural enactment, and "'reflect' on these lived-experiences, i.e., make these acts themselves and their immanent sense content into objects."[211] Reflection is thus characterized by the fact that we place ourselves outside the enactment of the lived-experience and the being-given-over to what is experienced that belongs to it – and then bend back to living-experience and thereby make this into the intentional object of the reflecting act. In the *natural* direction of enactment of lived-experiences, their experienced objects [74] are intuited and thought and "posited in any number of modalities of being as actualities."[212] In the *philosophical-phenomenological* attitude of thinking, "we should not

---

208 Husserl, *Logische Untersuchungen*, II/1, 9; *Huss.*, XIX/1,13; ET, 254f.
209 Ibid.
210 Ibid.
211 Ibid.
212 Ibid.

direct our theoretical interest to these objects [and] not posit *them* as actualities, as they appear and apply in the intention of those acts."[213] Rather, these acts, "which up to now were not objective at all," because they were experienced unthematically, "become the ob-jects of grasping and theoretical positing."[214] In the reflective acts of intuition and thinking we should "observe"[215] the objective, ob-jectified acts. In reflection and in accord with what is own to it, we should analyse, describe, make them [the objectified acts] into objects of an [...] ideative thinking."[216] The phenomenological description within the attitude of reflection is not an empirical but a pure description, because it aims for the essence of the acts. Husserl calls this pure description [*Beschreibung*] "description" [*Deskription*]. "Pure description" is "to be enacted" in the "unnatural *habitus* of reflection."[217] The transition from the pre-phenomenological into the phenomenological attitude is the "transition from the naïve enactment of the acts into the attitude of reflection, or into the enactment of the acts that belong to it."[218] Phenomenological reflection, then, is itself an intentional act whose intentional act-object is the otherwise experienced and now thematized act with its intentional relatedness to its act-object.

Basic executions regarding phenomenological reflection are to be found within *Ideas I*, "Considerations Fundamental to Phenomenology" (§§ 38 & 45) and then in the third section "Regarding Method and Problematic of Pure Phenomenology" (§§ 77–8).

[75] At the beginning of § 38, "Reflections on Acts, Immanent and Transcendent Perceptions,"[219] Husserl characterizes reflection in the same way as in *Logical Investigations*. Taking up the language of Descartes, Husserl says that as long as we live in the *cogito*, thus in lived-experience, "we do not have the *cogitatio* itself consciously as intentional object."[220] But the lived-experience can become an intentional object at any time. For "the fundamental possibility of a '*reflective directing of the*

---

213 Ibid.
214 Ibid.
215 Ibid., 10
216 Ibid.
217 Ibid., 11; *Huss.*, XIX/1, 16; ET, 256.
218 Ibid., 10.
219 Husserl, *Ideen I*, 67ff.; *Huss.*, III, 84.
220 Ibid., 67.

glance'"[221] belongs to the essence of lived-experience. This reflective directing of the glance is a "new *cogitatio*, one that aims at it straightforwardly."[222] The reflective directing of the glance is itself a *cogito*, an act, a lived-experience, which aims at the *cogito* that has been experienced unthematically up to now and which now makes it an intentional object. For its part, grasping in a straightforward manner, the act of reflection refers precisely to that *cogito*, just as it aims at its object as it grasps straightforwardly. Every *cogitatio*, every lived-experience, "can become object of a so-called 'inner perception.'"[223]

In § 45, "Unperceived Lived-Experience, Unperceived Reality,"[224] Husserl says of the manner of being of lived-experience, that belonging to it is the fact that "a glance of seeing perception can aim, totally and immediately, at every actual lived-experience that is alive as a primary presence,"[225] that is, as reflection. Reflection is thus *not* staying in the enactments of lived-experience, *not* understanding going-along with the trajectory of enactment of the lived-experiences, but rather a pulling back from this and a bending back of the glance to lived-experience, whereby this becomes an intentional object of the act of reflection.

But when a section on the methodology of pure phenomenology follows the "Considerations Fundamental to Phenomenology," one has to expect that here phenomenological reflection will be made thematic again, extensively. For our purposes we take up [76] only the fundamental characterizations. Already the title of § 77 signals the meaning of reflection for phenomenology: "Reflection as Fundamental Property of the Domain of Lived-Experience. Studies in Reflection."[226] Under the "most general essential properties of the pure domain of lived-experience," the first item to deal with, "for the sake of its *universal* methodological function," is "reflection."[227] The universal methodological function of reflection shows itself when "the phenomenological method" moves "entirely in acts of reflection."[228] The

---

221 Ibid.
222 Ibid.
223 Ibid.
224 Ibid., 83ff.
225 Ibid., 83.
226 Ibid., 144ff.
227 Ibid., 144.
228 Ibid.

"possibility of a phenomenology at all" rests in the "productive power of reflection."[229]

Once again the difference is drawn between living *in* the lived-experience and the reflecting gaze *at* the lived-experiences. "Every I experiences its lived-experiences."[230] Experiencing its lived-experiences does not mean that the I has these lived-experiences and what is determined in them thematically in view and that it grasps them in immanent perception. Experiencing its lived-experiences means to live in them in such a way that we live through them toward that to which we are pointed in experience. But every lived-experience that is lived through unthematically can "become something 'observed' in the ideal mode of possibility."[231] In this case a reflection is directed to what was before only a lived-through lived-experience, whereby this now becomes "object *for* the I."[232] But because reflections are also lived-experiences, the reflecting lived-experiences, for their part and through a reflection of a second level, can become their intentional object. The same applies to reflection as to every unreflected lived-experience. The reflecting I lives through the lived-experience of reflection without this lived-experience being thereby thematically in view. Only a further lived-experience of reflection, one that is directed to the reflecting lived-experience of the first level, makes this into an intentional ob-ject of the I. [77] "Study of the stream of lived-experience is enacted for its part in [...] reflective acts,"[233] which, because they themselves belong in the stream of lived-experience, "can, in corresponding reflections of a higher level, be made into ob-jects of phenomenological analyses."[234]

In § 78, "The Phenomenological Study of Reflections of Lived-Experiences," Husserl adheres to this: Reflection is a title for acts "in which the stream of lived-experience with all its manifold occurrences (moments of lived-experiences, intentionalities) becomes evidently graspable and analyzable."[235] Reflection is "the title for the method of consciousness for cognition of consciousness in general."[236] Not only

---

229 Ibid.
230 Ibid., 145.
231 Ibid.
232 Ibid.
233 Ibid., 147.
234 Ibid.
235 Ibid., 147.
236 Ibid.

the stream of lived-experience and its lived-experiences, but also reflection itself become, on the way of reflection, "ob-ject of possible studies."[237] Every reflection has the "character of a *modification of consciousness*," which "*every consciousness* can in principle experience."[238] Reflection is modification of consciousness, because it "in accord with its essence proceeds from out of a change of focus."[239] Through this reflective change of focus, an unreflected lived-experience experiences "a certain transformation":[240] it is transformed into reflected, ob-jectified consciousness. Every lived-experience can "be transferred into reflective modifications."[241] "All modes of immanent essential grasping"[242] fall under the concept of reflection.

The passages on the theme of phenomenological reflection from the *Logical Investigations* and *Ideas I*, which we have just brought to mind, form the textual background from which Heidegger, in the sections of the war emergency semester lectures already mentioned as well as those to follow, [78] speaks of the theoretical attitude and reflection as an objectification and ob-jectification. Objectification and ob-jectification in this context are not language creations of Heidegger, but direct recourses to Husserl.

(b) Heidegger's Method of Hermeneutic Understanding

The review of Husserl's pertinent passages on phenomenological reflection were preceded by a hermeneutic-phenomenological analysis of lived-experience of the surrounding world and of lived-experience of mere things. In retrospect on this analysis Heidegger recapitulates what we did *not* see in the hermeneutic looking-into these lived-experiences: nothing "psychic," no "ob-ject-domain that was merely meant [...] as specific, qualitatively outstanding region, i.e., psychic and not physical."[243] This "opposition of psychic and physical did not even show up in our [hermeneutic] field of vision."[244] For hermeneutic looking-into

237 Ibid.
238 Ibid., 148.
239 Ibid.
240 Ibid.
241 Ibid.
242 Ibid.
243 Heidegger, *Die Idee der Philosophie* ..., GA 56/57, 99.
244 Ibid.

both of those lived-experiences, there also did not appear "a mate-rial happening, i.e., we saw no processes."[245] Because right after this Heidegger lets some essential objections from Husserl's reflective phe-nomenology be articulated against the hermeneutic explanation, this defence is formulated above all with a view to Husserl. For herme-neutic seeing neither the lived-experience of the surrounding world nor the lived-experience of the thing is seen as psychic act over against physical act, because this designation and this difference belong nei-ther to a-theoretical experience nor to hermeneutic understanding of a-theoretical experience, but rather derive from the theoretical-reflective focus. For reflection the psychic is an ob-ject-domain, the domain of the intentional ob-ject of reflective acts. The psychic as intentional ob-ject is "meant" in the intentional [79] acts of reflection and prevails as what is reflectively meant. For hermeneutic seeing and understanding there are no ob-jects, no ob-ject-domain, because hermeneutic seeing does not reflect on lived-experiences, but rather goes along with the di-rection of enactment of lived-experiences, in understanding-interpreta-tion. What is hermeneutically interpreted is not ob-ject of hermeneutic interpretation, but rather the living experience itself, which has been made explicit and visible. It is only when interpretation becomes reflec-tion that the lived-experience appears as a psychic process that passes by in the immanent temporality of consciousness. In contrast to that, for hermeneutic interpretation the lived-experiences manifest as hap-penings [*Er-eignisse*] – not as intratemporal happenings [*Geschenisse*] but as the self-temporalizing experience that lives from within its own.

Now we will raise objections to this hermeneutic conclusion from out of reflective phenomenology. This counters: But we saw "something," the lived-experiences. The analytic seeing of lived-experiences can only mean: "We do not live any more in the lived-experiences, but rather look at them."[246] With this formulation the far-reaching difference be-tween the hermeneutic and the reflective interpretations breaks open. Phenomenological analyses of lived-experiences can only say that we stop the alive enactment of lived-experience in its living of what is experienced, in order to turn back and view the lived-experience from a new direction. For the one analysing, the lived-experience must attain the distance of the ob-ject meant, so that it can be analysed as

---

245 Ibid.
246 Ibid.

this lived-experience. Without this distance, into which the lived-experience is inserted by reflection, a phenomenological thematizing of lived-experience seems to be impossible. "Lived-experiences [as] experienced become [as] envisaged."[247] For the reflective focus the lived-experiences can be comprehended only in that which they are, when the one analysing steps out of the alive enactment of lived-experience and delivers the lived-experience to the opposite: the ob-ject to be investigated. Here Heidegger quotes [80] Husserl's key sentence – which we already know – from § 78 of *Ideas I*: "Through reflectively *experiencing* acts alone do we know anything of the stream of lived-experience."[248] Only through reflective acts can we make the stream of lived-experience and the lived-experiences that flow in those acts the theme of phenomenological analysis. These acts of reflection are "experiencing" acts because they bring the reflected lived-experience and its constituents to self-givenness. Acts of reflection are acts of reflective, mental intuition. Every lived-experience that is experienced and that stands in enactment "can become an envisaged experience, through turning one's look, through reflection."[249] Reflection is turning one's look, that is, the turning of a look from *what* is experienced in lived-experience to the lived-experience itself. To be able to interpret it as lived-experience, we must surrender the experiencing of the lived-experience; through the turning of the look, lived-experience must become an envisaged (reflected) object.

The second quotation from *Ideas I* comes from § 77: "The phenomenological method takes place entirely in reflection."[250] Reflection in the sense elucidated, and not in a general, lax sense, is the method of access to the domain of lived-experience. And because reflections are themselves lived-experiences, intentional lived-experiences, and because all lived-experiences can be reflectively objectified, then lived-experiences of reflection, which are at first experienced like other lived-experiences, but which are not seen as such, allow themselves to be seen and thus objectified in new experiences. For this issue as well Heidegger quotes from § 77 of *Ideas I*, in order to underscore the high importance that reflection occupies in Husserl's phenomenology.

---

247 Ibid.
248 Husserl, *Ideen I*, 150.
249 Heidegger, *Die Idee der Philosophie* ..., GA 56/57, 99.
250 *Ideen I*, 144.

Heidegger illustrates Husserl's phenomenological reflection with an experience of the thing. For this we are to transpose ourselves into such a lived-experience. As long as we live in this experience of the thing, we are oriented to the experienced thing. We describe the experienced thing, which is given as ob-ject, according to its extension, its color, its shape, and so on. Living in this description, [81] "the view of the 'I-consciousness' is directed to the thing."[251] That is the natural, pre-phenomenological, pre-reflective attitude. When the ray of vision of the I turns away from the thing experienced and directs itself to the experiencing and describing living-experience, we shift over to the reflective attitude. In this reflective turning of the look we extract the "field of lived-experience," the "stream of lived-experience,"[252] for a thematizing description. Not until we have reflected and only *through* reflection does the stream of lived-experience and every one of its lived-experiences become "describable."[253] With this, Heidegger brings to mind the descriptive character of phenomenology that was previously exhibited by Husserl in *Logical Investigations*. The phenomenological science of lived-experiences is a "descriptive" one. As such it is not empirical, but rather pure description, that is, a descriptive, describing eidetic doctrine of lived-experiences. But the essential description of lived-experiences is only possible as reflection. Heidegger lists various types of lived-experience: the lived-experiences of "perception," "memory," "presentation," "judgment," the you-experience, the they-experience, the we-experience, that is, types of person-experiences.[254] All of these become describable only through reflection in terms of their pure essence. Heidegger stresses that the phenomenological-reflective description does not imply that the lived-experiences are explained psychologically and refer back to physiological processes. Phenomenological description does not draw up hypotheses regarding the lived-experiences; rather, it exposes – "in straightforward measurement"[255] of what is brought reflectively to intuitive givenness – that "which lies as such in the lived-experiences."[256] In this way of proceeding, reflective

---

251 Heidegger, *Die Idee der Philosophie* ..., GA 56/57, 99.
252 Ibid.
253 Ibid., 100.
254 Ibid.
255 Ibid.
256 Ibid.

phenomenology follows its research-maxim, which is to return to the things themselves and only to approve as secured phenomenological knowledge that which [82] is itself drawn from the lived-experiences that have been brought to reflective givenness. Heidegger underscores this phenomenological way of proceeding in accord with the phenomenological research principle because this compliance is the one that hermeneutic phenomenology too makes its own, that is, it is what makes hermeneutics (in contrast to reflection) also phenomenology.

After Heidegger has sharply emphasized what is distinctive about the reflective access to the domain of lived-experience, with several quotations from *Ideas I*, he asks the deciding question: "Is this method of reflective description or describing reflection capable of investigating the domain of lived-experience, of disclosing it scientifically?"[257] Immediately after that he highlights what is decisive about reflection, in order to answer the question he has posed. "In the reflective turning of the look we make lived-experience, up to now not envisaged but only straightforwardly non-reflectively experienced, into something 'envisaged.'"[258] Phenomenological reflection is preceded by the "straightforward," that is, by the non-reflective living-experience [*Erleben*], which we undergo [*durchleben*] in one with the experienced. With this distinction Heidegger takes up the language of Husserl. "Experienced" here has two different meanings. "Every I experiences its lived-experiences,"[259] but not in such a way that the lived-experience itself is what is intentionally experienced. Thus we elucidate this "experiencing" [*erleben*] with the word "undergoing an experience" [*durchleben*]. But in the experienced, undergone lived-experiences, we experience something to which we are intentionally connected in the lived-experiences undergone. What is intentionally experienced dare not be confused with the experienced (undergone) lived-experiences. The experienced lived-experience is itself not in view, because it is undergone. What is in view is what we are intentionally connected to in the experienced lived-experience. Reflection that is now always possible is a reflective turning of the look, in which the look is thematically grasping as it points to lived-experience that up to now was non-reflectively experienced – and that makes out of a straightforwardly experienced lived-experience a reflectively seen one.

---

257 Ibid.
258 Ibid.
259 Husserl, *Ideen I*, 145.

[83] Now we no longer see primarily the experienced thing, in order to describe it. Instead we see the lived-experience of the thing in its intentional relatedness to the experienced [*erfahrenes*, i.e., undergone experience of] thing. "In reflection we have it standing there, are directed to it and make it into an ob-ject or object [*Objekt, Gegenstand*] in general."[260] In and through the reflective turning of the look, we no longer live in the lived-experience; rather, it "now stands there." "Standing there" indicates that the lived-experience is set aside from its living enactment. The livingness of the enactment is surrendered, in favour of a pure standing-there, because the lived-experience can apparently be phenomenologically interpreted only in this way of access. In reflection we are intentionally directed to the lived-experience, which before that was undergone in full aliveness. Lived-experience itself has become an intentional ob-ject or object through reflection. That alone is the sense of the phrase that Heidegger uses again and again, of ob-jectifying or objectifying. We do not understand this sense as long as Husserl's characterization of phenomenological reflection is unknown to us.

Reflecting on the lived-experience, having this there as seen, being intentionally directed to lived-experience, and thus making the lived-experience into an intentional ob-ject or object – all of this shows that in phenomenological reflection we are "theoretically focused."[261] "Theoretical" here does not mean this or that theory, but literally: observing. To this *observing* belongs the *distance* from what is observed, which itself shifts into the *over-against* of observing. By means of this modification the lived-experience loses what is its own, the wholly living character of enactment. Thus this theoretical attitude of phenomenological reflection is one that is "stripping of life [*entlebend*]."[262] The theoretical attitude of reflection withdraws from the pre-theoretical living-experience of the pre-theoretical aliveness that is own to it. To this aliveness there belong specific characteristics of lived-experience that are closed off by the reflective-theoretical [84] scanning. Lived-experience does still manifest itself in reflection, but in a way other than one that does not make the pre-theoretical character of lived-experience disappear but rather brings it straight to a phenomenological showing. How reflection strips lived-experiences of life shows itself clearly in the language itself, by

---

260 Heidegger, *Die Idee der Philosophie* ..., GA 56/57, 100.
261 Ibid.
262 Ibid.

the fact that lived-experiences in reflection are "no longer experienced" but rather "envisaged."[263] Reflective seeing includes the withdrawal of living and living-experience. In this withdrawal the a-theoretical *Ereignis* character of lived-experiences is closed off.

In phenomenological reflection we place the lived-experiences in the over-against. But to "place" them thus means to place them outside "immediate living-experience."[264] The answer to the question posed above can now be given. The question read: "Is this method of reflective description or describing reflection capable of investigating the domain of lived-experience, of disclosing it scientifically?" The answer is: No. But first and right away a Yes must be placed alongside this No. For on the one hand the phenomenological method of reflective description is very well capable of disclosing the domain of lived-experience scientifically. One needs here only a reference to the work on phenomenology done by Husserl. The method of descriptive reflection is capable of *theoretically* disclosing the universal domain of lived-experience. What is theoretically disclosed in this manner has its own truth in itself.

Heidegger's question whether the method of descriptive reflection is capable of disclosing the domain of lived-experience scientifically does not deny the fact that this method is indeed capable of doing this. Heidegger does not question whether that method can disclose the domain of lived-experience at all. Rather, the question is whether the method of descriptive reflection is capable of disclosing the domain of lived-experience in its *a-theoretical* character. When asked in this way, the question must be answered in the negative. For if there is actually an a-theoretical domain of living and living-experience [85] that is to be phenomenologically disclosed in its pre-theoretical character, then it needs another way of access, and not that of reflection. For by means of the access of reflection the pre-theoretical character is precisely closed off – and can no longer be recovered by way of reflective description. The method or way of access that is set over against descriptive reflection is hermeneutic seeing and understanding. This gets its life from the insight that there is something a-theoretical and that this can be made phenomenologically thematic and visible only when we do not lift lived-experiences out of immediate living-experience, but rather stay right in this immediate living-experience – in such a way, of course, that

---

263 Ibid.
264 Ibid.

we bring this into expression. Hermeneutic seeing and understanding does not modify the lived-experiences in lifting them out of the living enactment of lived-experience and placing them in the over-against of intentional object; instead, in going-along with the immediate living-experience, it shifts it from pre-phenomenological unexpressedness into phenomenological explicitness. Only in this way does hermeneutic understanding not deprive lived-experiences of their own character; rather, it preserves that character in order to reveal it as such.

The a-theoretical procedure of hermeneutic seeing must be set off from the theoretical procedure of descriptive reflection – which is not to say that the theoretical procedure is false. Also, hermeneutic phenomenology must stress that the pre-theoretical, which it privileges, is closed off by the method of reflection. It even has to go so far as to designate its methodological procedure as one that comprehends the phenomenological investigation-maxim "to the things themselves" more radically than reflective phenomenology. But it cannot and will not set itself up as absolute, as if there were only one way of phenomenology, namely this one. Hermeneutic, a-theoretical phenomenology and reflective, theoretical phenomenology are two ways, each appropriate in its own way.

[86]

§ 7. The Phenomenological "Principle of Principles"

The "fundamental methodological problem of phenomenology" in general – for reflexive as well as for hermeneutic phenomenology – is "the question of the manner of scientific disclosure of the domain of lived-experience."[265] But this question comes "under the 'principle of principles.'"[266] Regarding this fundamental phenomenological principle, formulated by Husserl in *Ideas I*, Heidegger shows that it is not itself of a theoretical nature, even though it has been established by Husserl for reflective phenomenology. Before we turn to Heidegger's interpretation of this principle, it is incumbent upon us first to interpret the principle in the version that Husserl gives it.

---

265 Ibid., 109.
266 Ibid.

(a) Reflective-Phenomenological Intuition (Husserl)

It is § 24 from the first section of *Ideas I*, "Essence and Essential Cognition," that is entitled "The Principle of Principles."[267] The full formulation reads: "that *every originarily presentive [gebend] intuition is a legitimate source for cognition, that everything* that *is offered* to us *originarily in 'intuition'* (as it were, in its corporeal actuality) *is simply to be accepted as that which is given,* but also *only within the limits in which it is given.*"[268] At the end of § 23 we read: "But grasping and intuition of essences is a polymorphic act, especially *seeing essences is an originarily presentive act* and as such the *analogue of sense perceiving.*"[269] Here the phenomenological seeing of essences – that is, seeing the essence (*eidos*) of lived-experiences as an "originarily presentive act" – is designated as a counterpart to sense perceiving. Therefore, sense perception is the model for that which is called "originarily presentive [giving]." [87] Sense perception is an originarily presentive lived-experience, because it makes the perceived thing originarily, primordially *given*, but that means "in its corporeal actuality." The originary givenness of something is its corporeal givenness. By contrast, an act of making-present [*Vergegenwärtigung*] – for example, making-present of the present – indeed offers the object itself as made-present (and not only an objectifying image [*Vorstellungsbild*] of it), but not in its corporeal actuality. Analogous to sense perception and its originarily presentive intuiting, the psychic apprehension of essences is also an originarily presentive intuition – of course, not a sensory but a psychic intuition – in which the phenomenological essence of a lived-experience is seen [*erschaut*] and offered as corporeally seen.

Now that we have clarified what "originarily presentive intuition" in the realm of sensory and of psychic intuiting means, we can turn to the "principle of principles." "Every" originarily presentive intuition – not only the sensory, but also corresponding to it, the psychic intuition – is originarily a giving intuition, which offers what is intuited originarily, that is, in its sensory or psychic corporeal actuality. Not only the sensorily, originarily giving intuition but also the psychic, originarily giving intuition is "a legitimate source for cognition." Just as a sense cognition

---

267 Husserl, *Ideen I*, § 24, 43ff.
268 Ibid.
269 Ibid.

gains its legitimacy from the fact that sense perceiving offers what is perceived in its corporeal actuality, so does a psychic cognition of essences gain its legitimacy from the fact that it is a psychic intuiting that offers the psychically seen originarily, corporeally. Husserl calls psychic intuition also "in-tuition." Everything "that is offered to us in 'intuition,'" in psychic intuition, "originarily (as it were, in its corporeal actuality)" is to be "simply accepted" by the phenomenologist "as it is given." What is psychically originarily intuited is to be cognitively accepted as the phenomenological, as that which is shown in the originarily giving psychic intuition, without any intervening theory. Delineated more sharply, what gives itself originarily, corporeally, in the psychic intuition may be taken in "also only within the limits" [88] in which the seen is given. For there exists the danger that we will add something to what is given originarily – regardless from what source – that does not belong to the corporeally given. The psychic intuition of the phenomenologist is phenomenological in-tuition. Every other meaning that we couple with the word *in-tuition* must be switched off, here in the space of phenomenology.

With this principle of all principles "no conceivable theory can confound us." The principle of all principles cannot be put into question by means of any theory, because every theory must "draw" its own truth "again only from out of the originary givenness."[270] The principle of all principles is not itself a theory. Rather, it is that methodologically fundamental principle that enables the truth of every theory. The principle of all principles is "an *absolute beginning*," a "*principium*,"[271] for all genuine theory.

The methodologically fundamental principle formulates the methodological maxim that all phenomenological investigation must follow: heeding the fact that the cognitions that are displayed by it are based on the originarily giving intuition, that is, in-tuition, and that only what is given originarily in in-tuition may be given out as phenomenological cognition. But what is originarily self-given is nothing other than the self-showing of the things [*Sachen*] themselves. It thus becomes clear: the principle of all principles is nothing other than the already often-named phenomenological research-maxim "going back to the things themselves" and "going to the things themselves." Husserl established

---

270 Ibid., 44.
271 Ibid.

this maxim for the first time in § 2 of the Introduction to the second volume of *Logical Investigations*. He repeated it in § 19 of *Ideas I*: "But to judge things rationally or scientifically means to orient oneself to the *things themselves*, or to go back from the discourses and opinions to the things themselves, to question them in their self-givenness, and to set aside all prejudices that are alien to the things."[272] The phenomeno-logical investigation-maxim [89] "going back to the things themselves" and the phenomenological principle of all principles, the challenge to intuition-cognition, aim at the specific methodology of the phenomeno-logical method. To return to the things themselves means to return to the originarily giving in-tuition, in which in each case the thing to be cognized phenomenologically is given to cognition in corporeal actual-ity. Phenomenological cognition for Husserl is a returning to the things themselves, which can only be cognized if they are given or shown in psychic in-tuition.

(b) Hermeneutic-Phenomenological In-tuition (Heidegger)

The question of the *manner* of scientific disclosure of the domain of lived-experience comes under the methodological principle of all principles, which coincides with the phenomenological investigation-maxim "go-ing back to the things themselves." Phenomenology is defined *as* phe-nomenology through the principle of all principles. Thus this principle suits Heidegger as well. But that is possible only if this methodologi-cal fundamental principle is not of a theoretical nature from the start. Had Husserl, within his reflective phenomenology – in a reflective way of seeing – enunciated this in itself non-theoretical principle, then the reflective mantle would have had to be deflected, so that only the non-theoretical core of this principle would be taken into account. These considerations guide Heidegger in his interpretive appropriation of the principle of all principles.

Heidegger takes up the principle of all principles in shortened form: "*Everything* that is *offered originarily* [...] *in in-tuition* [is] *simply to be ac-cepted ... as that which it is.*"[273] This abbreviation of the entire passage that we quoted above, from § 24 of *Ideas I*, shows what is decisive for him from this principle. Phenomenological seeing must be enacted as

---

272 Ibid., 35.
273 Heidegger, *Die Idee der Philosophie ...*, GA 56/57, 109.

phenomenological in-tuition [90], in which what is to be seen is originarily offered. What is thus offered/given originarily is to be accepted
without any consideration pushed in between. Interpretation of what
is offered in in-tuition must keep strictly to what shows itself. Thereby
we have already given to the principle of all principles a formulation
that is binding, not only for reflective but also for hermeneutic phenomenology. Heidegger then notes a significant addition in Husserl's own
text, that with this principle of all principles "no conceivable theory can
confound us."[274] This addition by Husserl indicates that the principle
itself is not a theory and also that no theory is capable of putting this
principle into question, because any such theory would have to "draw"
its own truth from out of "originary givennesses" and thereby itself
remains relegated to this principle.

However, is not talk of a "principle" itself theory? Is the principle of
all principles not already a theoretical proposition? If it were a theoretical proposition, "then the term would not be congruent,"[275] – the term
"principle of all principles." This term is congruent only if the "principle" is something "that precedes all principles."[276] These principles,
ahead of which the "principle" of all principles lies, could be theoretical
sentences. But with this one principle, ahead of which the "principle"
of all principles lies, "no conceivable theory can confound." But that
means that this principle is itself "not of a theoretical nature,"[277] not
a theoretical sentence, which would demand for its assertion and its
truth the return to originary givenness. The "principle" of all principles
is not a supreme theoretical sentence from which all other theoretical
sentences derive; rather, it is *principium* in the sense of absolute beginning of all phenomenological knowledge.

But did we not say, again and again, that phenomenological seeing,
and thus Husserl's intuition, is of a reflective nature? Husserl [91] formulates the principle of all principles for reflective phenomenology. For
Husserl phenomenological in-tuition is reflective in-tuition. Everything
reflective belongs to the theoretical. The discourse of the theoretical
does not mean only a theory in the sense of one or several theoretical sentences. By theoretical Heidegger means above all the reflective

---

274 Ibid.
275 Ibid.
276 Ibid.
277 Ibid.

objectifying encounter with what is pre-reflective. The principle of all principles may well not be a theoretical sentence itself; it could still be of a theoretical nature in the sense that originarily presentive intuition, or in-tuition, is nothing other than reflective in-tuition. If that were the case, then hermeneutic phenomenology would also have to distance itself from this principle.

However, for Heidegger, when the principle of all principles is kept free of its reflective explanation, not only is it not a theoretical sentence, but also in its core it is not bound to reflection. There is a threefold characterization of this principle: "It is the primordial intention of true living in general, the primordial attitude of living-experience and living as such, the absolute *sympathy with living* that is identical with living-experience itself."[278]

It is the primordial intention of true living in general to take in what is experienced in living-experience in such a way that the surrounding world that is experienced in this living-experience is given originally in the seeing of living-experience. Living-experience allows what comes to meet us in lived-experience to be encountered without theoretical scanning. Allowing something to be encountered is therefore just as a-theoretical as that which encounters it. That is the primordial intention of true living and living-experience. It is this primordial intention that phenomenology reaches for when it turns the pre-theoretical living-experience of what is encountered from naive unexpressedness into phenomenological explicitness. But phenomenology thus understood in its seeing, in its in-tuition, is hermeneutic phenomenology. Therefore, the principle of all principles – looked at correctly – names the way of proceeding of phenomenology as hermeneutic phenomenology. Seen from this perspective, reflective phenomenology would be a deviation from the [92] hermeneutic tendency that resides in the principle of all principles. Hermeneutic phenomenology does not interrupt the primordial intention of living and living-experience in order to objectify it reflectively, but rather embraces the primordial intention in order to make it phenomenologically clear and distinct and transparent. The principle of all principles "is" the primordial intention of life, in that life takes the primordial intention on, untouched by the theoretical, and, going-along with it, makes it explicit.

---

278 Ibid., 110.

Insofar as the principle of all principles follows the primordial intention of true living, it is "the primordial attitude of living-experience and living as such." It "is" this primordial attitude, in that it embraces it, goes along with it, and interprets it in understanding. Phenomenology that follows the principle of all principles does not abandon this primordial attitude of living-experience in order to switch into the attitude of reflection. Instead, it remains in this primordial attitude, although not in a pre-philosophical manner, but rather now in a philosophical-phenomenological manner.

When the principle of all principles embraces the primordial intention and the primordial attitude of living-experience, it is "the absolute *sympathy with living* that is identical with living-experience itself." Because hermeneutic phenomenology goes along with living and living-experience and its a-theoretical intention – and only in this way interprets living-experience – it and its methodological fundamental principle are the absolute sympathy with living and living-experience. The sympathy is co-living-experience, the concurrence of phenomenological seeing with living-experience and living in the mode of explicitness. The word *sympathy with living* is the hermeneutic counter-word to reflection, which interrupts the primordial intention of living-experience in order to analyse the living-experience from out of reflective ob-jectifying.

The hermeneutic-phenomenological fundamental attitude of absolute – that is, not limited – sympathy with living in full explicitness must be cultivated and exercised as a methodologically fundamental attitude. Phenomenological living is not captured by means of artifice, but requires "growing intensification."[279] The "primordial habitus of the phenomenologist," here the [93] hermeneutic phenomenologist, "cannot be appropriated quickly."[280] The primordial habitus of absolute sympathy with living "becomes [mere] form and leads to occlusion of all genuine problems, if it is handled merely mechanically, in the manner of a routine."[281]

From within this methodological fundamental attitude, which expresses itself in the principle of all principles and in its interpretation as absolute sympathy with living, phenomenology achieves its own

---

279 Ibid.
280 Ibid.
281 Ibid.

"rigour" and its "scientific character."[282] It is rigorously scientific when it knows that the things themselves – to which it wants to give the first and last word – manifest themselves in the primordial intention and primordial attitude of living and living-experience and in the absolute sympathy with living. Hermeneutic phenomenology is rigorously scientific when its in-tuition keeps entirely to what is originarily offered. Of course, not only hermeneutic phenomenology but also reflective phenomenology get their scientific rigour from following the principle of all principles. In both ways of phenomenology "the methodological problem has a central position ... like no other science,"[283] because phenomenological in-tuition as method must always be appropriated anew and kept alive.

Phenomenology can be "preserved only through itself,"[284] without the aid of a philosophical standpoint that is itself not of phenomenological origin. Every "aid [is] a sin against its own spirit."[285] Philosophical standpoints are, for example, realism and idealism. In *Ideas I* it says of phenomenology that it takes its "opening from what lies *before* all standpoints: from the whole realm of what is given intuitively and still prior to all theoretical thinking."[286] Heidegger sharpens [94] phenomenology's lack of standpoint in this formulation: "And the *mortal sin* would be the opinion that *it itself is a standpoint.*"[287]

Phenomenology completely and only invokes seeing and in-tuition, the in-tuition of what is originarily offered in it. But phenomenology is at the same time description, description of what is seen phenomenologically. Now, that is formulated so broadly that it applies to both hermeneutic and reflective phenomenology. One could object that what is seen phenomenologically is nonetheless theorized again, by means of the description. If one grants that phenomenological seeing must not be of a theoretical nature, then what is seen pre-theoretically appears to be handled theoretically through description. Can a hermeneutic phenomenology be carried out in such a way that it is of an a-theoretical nature, not only in its primary in-tuition but also in its description and formulation in language? Phenomenological description and formulation in

---

282 Ibid.
283 Ibid.
284 Ibid.
285 Ibid.
286 Husserl, *Ideen I*, 38.
287 Heidegger, *Die Idee der Philosophie...*, GA 56/57, 110.

language might have a theoretical character in itself, if description and formulation were of a reflective nature. Must description and formulation be carried out as and in reflection?

Phenomenological seeing, phenomenological in-tuition, would be a reflective seeing, if it "stands over against or (as something depicted)" stood "outside itself."[288] But it is precisely "hidden theory to stamp the domain of lived-experience as a given,"[289] given in the over-against of phenomenological seeing. Reflective seeing stands *outside* what is to be seen, whereas hermeneutic seeing stands *within* what is to be seen. For hermeneutic in-tuition – precisely *other than* for reflective in-tuition – there does not exist "this duality and pulling apart [95] of object and knowledge, of what is given (to be given) and description."[290] The duality and pulling apart of phenomenological seeing and what is to be seen follows from reflection, which does not stay within what is to be seen, but rather stands outside and over against it. In contrast, hermeneutic seeing stays within that which is to be seen by it in the sense of absolute sympathy with living. Not only seeing, but also phenomenological describing and formulating of what is originarily seen, stay within what is seen, what is to be described, and what is to be formulated. Hermeneutic description and language-giving, too, take place in absolute sympathy with living and are thus not of a theoretical but rather of an a-theoretical nature.

Hermeneutic-phenomenological seeing takes place as a going-along with living, as absolute sympathy with living and living-experience. With a view to this way of proceeding of hermeneutic seeing, Heidegger outlines hermeneutic-phenomenological in-tuition as demarcated from reflective-phenomenological in-tuition: "The experiencing of living-experience that is appropriating and carries itself along-with is *hermeneutic in-tuition* in understanding."[291] Hermeneutic in-tuition is an experiencing of living-experience. Reflective in-tuition, too, would let itself be grasped as experiencing the living-experience. But here living-experience is reflection, a reflecting living-experience that does not stay within what is to be experienced live, does not go along with this, but rather keeps outside what is to be experienced live, so that this forms

---

288 Ibid., 111.
289 Ibid.
290 Ibid., 111f.
291 Ibid., 117.

its over-against. By contrast, hermeneutic in-tuition is a seeing living-experience, which carries itself along with the lived-experience to be seen. In explicitly going-along with the lived-experience to be understood, this lived-experience is made explicit with its immediate enactment-orientation. Hermeneutic living-experience of the lived-experience to be understood is "appropriating," in that it is appropriated in explicit accompaniment with the lived-experience of this lived-experience. [96] Lived-experience is not ob-jectified through this appropriating. For hermeneutic appropriating is not reflection, but rather a making-explicit of the lived-experiences to be understood, by going-along with them. Hermeneutic in-tuition is not reflection on living, but "the understanding of living."[292] The phenomenological as hermeneutic in-tuition is in-tuition that "makes understandable and is sense-giving."[293] It makes living and living-experience understandable, in that it goes along with it and in this accompanying makes lived-experience explicit.

Although for reflective phenomenology's way of viewing, the originarily presentive in-tuition is reflective intuition, the principle of all principles, that is, the challenge of an originarily presentive in-tuition, does not arise from reflection. The same principle of all principles can be the fundamental principle for phenomenological reflection as well as for phenomenological hermeneutics. Reflection and hermeneutics are phenomenology by their common sharing of the principle of all principles. And because this principle coincides with the phenomenological investigation-maxim "going back to the things themselves," reflective and hermeneutic phenomenology hold this maxim in common.

Originarily giving in-tuition is on the one hand reflective, on the other hand hermeneutic, in-tuition. For reflective in-tuition the life of consciousness presents itself with its lived-experiences of consciousness. For the understanding, hermeneutic in-tuition, what shows itself is the a-theoretical domain of lived-experience with its a-theoretical lived-experiences of the surrounding world. It does not show itself in the over-against of reflective ob-jectification, but rather in explicitly understanding going-along with the orientation of lived-experience. For reflective in-tuition, as the fundamental layer of the life of consciousness, what show themselves are the lived-experiences of sense experience [*Erfahrung*], which are the basis of everything and in which the material

---

292 Heidegger, *Die Idee der Philosophie…*, 219.
293 Ibid.

corporeality of the world is known [*bewußt*] as the basis. By contrast, for hermeneutic in-tuition what shows itself as the fundamental layer of a-theoretical living are the lived-experiences of the surrounding world, the understanding living-experience of the surrounding world in [97] its respective significance, by which it belongs to the surrounding world as a significance-whole.

In the war emergency lecture course, reflective phenomenology is transformed into hermeneutic phenomenology. The "hermeneutic turn in phenomenology" does not somehow say that the hermeneutics that had already existed prior to the establishing of phenomenology is now introduced into phenomenology. In the establishing of hermeneutic phenomenology, the essence of the hermeneutic is grounded anew. All older hermeneutics share in the dominance of the theoretical – thus hermeneutics is handled theoretically – whereas Heidegger establishes the sense of an a-theoretical hermeneutics, through first discovering a-theoretical living and living-experience.

The discovery of the a-theoretical domain of living and living-experience and the accompanying establishment of hermeneutic phenomenology is the decisive beginning of a way that moves through the subsequent early Freiburg and Marburg lecture courses and culminates in *Being and Time*. Hermeneutic in-tuition further guides the science of the origin of factical life, the hermeneutics of facticity, and the hermeneutic phenomenology of Dasein. Everything that Heidegger expresses regarding formal indication [*formale Anzeige*] belongs to hermeneutic phenomenology.

When hermeneutic phenomenology of factical life becomes ontology in terms of thematics, what is involved is not an ontological turning, as if ontological questions are initially excluded from the hermeneutics of factical life. Above all, the formulation of ontological questions does not at all mean penetration of the theoretical into the a-theoretical domain. The primordial science of a-theoretical living and the science of the origin of factical life ("a-theoretical" and "factical" coincide) are not established with the intention of abandoning the traditional fundamental questions of philosophy. The basic questions of philosophy about being, world, space, time, and truth are not theoretical questions from the start; rather, they are [98] merely taken up and carried out in theoretical-reflective fashion in traditional philosophy, which is based on the dominance of the theoretical. Philosophy as a-theoretical primordial science of a-theoretical living and living-experience, which as such is hermeneutic phenomenology, prepares the way for asking the fundamental questions of philosophy in a new, a-theoretical way of seeing. These fundamental questions are not brought in, as it were, from the outside *into* the a-theoretical domain of living and living-experience; rather, they should and must be asked on the hermeneutic-phenomenological pathway into the all-inclusive a-theoretical domain and from within this domain.

Hermeneutic phenomenology of Dasein in *Being and Time* is the opening of the a-theoretical domain – which now carries the name *Dasein* – in order, from within the a-theoretical Dasein-domain, to get to the clues for the a-theoretical fundamental questions of philosophy. The program of *Being and Time* must be read entirely in this a-theoretical hermeneutic point of view.

But not only that. The transition from the transcendental-horizonal to the enowning-historical way of seeing – and the thoughts attained in this way of seeing – must be carried out along with and from within the sustaining a-theoretical-hermeneutic point of view. To the very end of his philosophical life, in his conversations, Heidegger held fast to the non-reflective character of being-historical thinking. But at the beginning of his own pathway of thinking, in the war emergency semester lecture course, he developed what the non-reflective says as the a-theoretical of hermeneutic phenomenology. Philosophical thinking is a-theoretical-hermeneutic when it does not bring what is to be thought into the over-against of reflection, but rather goes along with the experiencing living, with Dasein that understands being, and with en-owned Dasein – and lifts this out of the pre-phenomenological un-expressedness into phenomenological explicitness.

Part Two

Husserl–Heidegger and "the Things Themselves"

[101]

§ 1. The Phenomenological Maxim "To the Things Themselves" and Overcoming Prejudice

In the winter semester of 1923–4, Heidegger began his Marburg teaching appointment with the lecture course "Introduction to Phenomenological Research,"[294] motivated by the intention *"to understand and to further phenomenology as possibility."*[295] For Heidegger, phenomenology as method finds expression solely in the maxim coined by Husserl: "to the things themselves." The emphasis on the *possibility-character* of phenomenology indicates that the interpretation that Husserl gave to this maxim is only *one* possibility of what phenomenology as a philosophizing that is determined by the self-giving of the things can be. In Husserl's phenomenology this one possibility has *de facto* become descriptive, eidetic science of transcendentally pure consciousness. In view of this, the question arises whether this interpretation of phenomenology is commensurate with the methodological principle in the way that things themselves are *truly released* in order to be able to confront us freely from themselves. Thus, with respect to the maxim, Heidegger requires "concern for an instinct-secure overcoming of prejudice."[296] This

---

294 Heidegger, *Einführung in die phänomenologische Forschung*, GA 17, 1994.
295 Ibid., 263.
296 Ibid., 2.

does not mean lacking all preconception, but rather "overcoming every possibility that anything emerges as a prejudice,"[297] being free "for the possibility of letting go of any prejudice, in the deciding moment from within and out of coming to terms with the thing."[298] Of special importance is the addition that this surpassing of prejudice is "the form of existence of scientific man."[299] In accord with this, it does not suffice in phenomenology [102] "if one invokes a mere looking at and dedication to the things."[300] For it could be "that all of that is burdened with an enormous number of preconceptions: In order to come *to the things themselves*, they must be *released*."[301] "The most perverse dogmatism" can be "hidden" behind the maxim "to the things themselves."[302] For Heidegger the phenomenological principle suffers the loss of its *radical tendency* through the *Husserlian interpretation*, which does not truly open the way to the things themselves, but rather obstructs it.[303] Husserl's interpretation of what the things themselves are is an *assumption* that alone governs how the things themselves are to attain their self-giving. Heidegger recognizes this assumption as a *preconception*, which, in the sense of overcoming prejudice as required by the maxim, must be given up. But the insight into this preconception becomes possible only because the ability of things to present themselves freely has already been shown – and it is this being-able that is stifled by the Husserlian interpretation. *Heidegger's answer to Husserl's Freiburg phenomenology*[304] grows out of his *more radical* take on the *phenomenological maxim*. What is the interpretation, exposed by Heidegger as preconception, that Husserl gives to the phenomenological principle? How does Husserl determine the things themselves? To what extent does this determination prevent the things themselves from being-able to freely confront us? What are the things themselves for Heidegger?

---

297 Ibid.
298 Ibid.
299 Ibid.
300 Ibid., 275.
301 Ibid.
302 Ibid., 60.
303 Ibid., 278
304 [Translator's note: The reference to "Husserl's Freiburg phenomenology" is to distinguish it from his "Halle phenomenology," that is, the phenomenology of the *Logical Investigations*.]

§ 2. Consciousness and Preoccupation with Cognized Cognition

In order to make comprehensible the things that phenomenology deals with – the kind of things that Husserlian phenomenology deals with – Heidegger starts with a designation of the things that stand in the field of vision of Aristotle and thus [103] of Greek philosophy. There is on the one hand the *being of the world* and on the other hand *life* as *being in a world*. Whereas the being of the world has the character of self-showing (φαινόμενον), the being of life is determined by a fundamental possibility of showing the being of the world through speaking (λόγος). At the same time, the being of the world in its self-showing has the possibility of merely masquerading-as, just as life has the possibility of obscuring, in speaking, the world that is there.[305] That means for Heidegger that the Greek interpretation of Dasein remains "within Dasein," that it is Dasein itself, insofar as it becomes expressed through explication.

In contrast to this, the orientation of Husserl's phenomenological view (and, even before that, the view of modern philosophy) has been turned around. It is guided *"by the predominance of an empty and thereby fantastical idea of certainty and evidence."*[306] This predominance is one that is *"prior to every intrinsic release of being-able to present themselves that belongs to the actual things of philosophy."*[307] *"Preoccupation with* a definitively *absolute cognition*, taken purely as idea, assumes predominance before every question of [the] things."[308] The *idea* of a definite *cognition* determines the theme, instead of the other way around, that is, that "a determinate *condition of things* allocates the possibilities for scientific work."[309]

It is the predominant idea of absolute certainty and cognition that lets *consciousness* become the field of focus for phenomenology. Priority of the focal point of "consciousness" – and with that the priority of the idea of absolute certainty – is now interpreted by Heidegger in terms of "intrinsic *possibilities* that *Dasein* carries in itself."[310] But with this it

---

305 Ibid., 44.
306 Ibid., 43.
307 Ibid.
308 Ibid.
309 Ibid., 44. [Emphasis by von Herrmann.]
310 Ibid., 47.

becomes clear that now, alongside the Aristotle-interpretation, above all the Husserl-interpretation as well is enacted with a view to Dasein, that setting up [104] consciousness as the field of focus for absolute cognition is a way in which Dasein comports itself to itself. It is that way of being of Dasein in which Dasein betakes itself to the possibility of letting itself be encountered for self-interpretation, without concealment.

But before Heidegger turns to the Dasein-oriented interpretation of phenomenology of transcendentally purified consciousness, he acknowledges the *breakthrough of phenomenology* in Husserl's *Logical Investigations*. Although these investigations are traditional – in that they are oriented to logic and epistemology – what is *originary and striking* in them is that they formulate for the first time the investigation-maxim "to the things themselves" and, accordingly, *actually work on the things themselves*, on the thematic objects, in such a way that they bring these things to self-showing, as they are in themselves.[311] Among all of Husserl's writings, it is the *Logical Investigations* – notwithstanding their traditional framework – that dedicate themselves totally to the things themselves, without veering into the predominance of the modern idea of absolute certainty and cognition; for this reason, Heidegger gave unqualified preference to these texts. It was the *Logical Investigations* on which he practised phenomenological seeing, in the private seminar he held every Saturday from 1920 to 1923. For in the phenomenological analyses of the fifth and sixth of the *Logical Investigations*, one can learn how seeing also works for hermeneutic-phenomenological primordial science of factical life – the primordial science that Heidegger was engaged in already in his development in 1919.

After pointing out the breakthrough in phenomenological research that is made in *Logical Investigations*, Heidegger turns to phenomenology's *development*, specifically to the question of how far the [105] phenomenological research-attitude established in *Logical Investigations* "is maintained and how far it is warped or in the end lets the attitude in its decisive meaning slip away."[312] Instead of examining in detail Husserl's development of transcendental phenomenology, especially in *Ideas I*,[313]

---

311 Heidegger, *Einführung in die phänomenologische Forschung*, GA 17, 50.
312 Ibid., 1.
313 Husserl, *Ideen zu einer reinen Phänomenologie und phänomenologischen Philosophie, Erstes Buch: Allgemeine Einführung in die reine Phänomenologie; Huss.*, III.

Heidegger turns to the essay *Philosophy as Rigourous Science* (1911)[314] in order to listen to Husserl's continuing work there, "where *it speaks from itself* … where it expresses itself critically over against contemporary philosophy."[315] For this critique, "in its very manner against that which it resists, shows that to which it points." *Husserl's critique* is directed against *naturalism* and against *historicism* in philosophy, both of which threaten the idea of philosophy as rigorous science. Naturalism says that the "way of being and of the object of the nature-relationship" becomes "the substantive guide for comprehending being and objectivity *of any kind*."[316] For every aspect of being and its epistemological determination, the "specific rigour of mathematical natural science"[317] is authoritative. The *"extension* of a definite *idea of science and of the object* in the direction of the thematic field of philosophy"[318] takes place when it comes to *"naturalizing of consciousness"*[319] as well as *"naturalizing of ideas."*[320] Naturalizing of consciousness says that the psychic being, placed as nature, [106] is defined in the sense of scientific categories. But with that the ideal laws concerning the ways of lawfulness of pure processes of consciousness are reinterpreted, as are the valid norms in the laws of psychological processes. Naturalizing of ideas means that the specific lawfulness of sense and its validity is reinterpreted into a lawfulness of the natural process of the operation of thinking and that the norm and lawfulness of ideas is reinterpreted into a lawfulness of the course of thinking. The critique that Husserl designates as *clarifying the problem* is directed against the naturalizing of consciousness and of ideas, "in order to attain a *genuine science of consciousness.*"[321] But what is decisive for Heidegger is that this critical clarifying makes absolute "precisely the *intention* and *the idea of a scientific working out of consciousness*" as it exists in naturalism.[322] What matters for Husserl in this clarifying is to purge the field of consciousness of every naturalistic factuality, in order to achieve the foundation for philosophy as rigorous

---

314 Husserl, *Philosophie als strenge Wissenschaft* in *Huss.*, XXV, 3–62.
315 Heidegger, *Einführung in die phänomenologische Forschung*, GA 17, 60.
316 Ibid., 64.
317 Ibid.
318 Ibid.
319 Ibid., 65.
320 Ibid., 66.
321 Ibid., 71.
322 Ibid.

science. In this tendency to purge, Heidegger sees "the *preoccupation with securing cognition* on the way to cognizing cognition, [for the sake of] *securing and grounding an absolute scientificality*."[323] In the Husserlian critique of naturalism all those moments are eliminated "that can threaten the achievement of an *absolute evidence* and *certitude*."[324] The purging has two aspects. First, it is the *transcendental* purging, in which consciousness is liberated from every impurity of natural positions. But since the transcendentally purged consciousness is still an individual and unique flow of lived-experience, it still requires the *eidetic* purging in order to achieve essential cognition with reference to consciousness, in rigorously intersubjective validity. This twofold purging shows the *preoccupation with absolute binding forces, absolute scientificality*. Also belonging to this preoccupation is the *interest in discipline*, ending up at the *fundamental discipline* of philosophy: *absolute* [107] *science* as transcendental phenomenology of pure consciousness, which for its part is stipulated as unity of disciplines. Philosophy is apprehended as science of norms and of values. Characteristic of this preoccupation with known cognition is the prevailing of absolute scientificality, absolute cognition and its certitude, *prior to* a possibility of freely encountering the things themselves. The things themselves must submit from the very beginning to that idea of scientificality and cognition. Also belonging to Husserl's conception of philosophy as rigorous science is the *predominant guide* of the class of lived-experiences of *theoretical cognizing*, in accompaniment with which the structure of all relationships to lived-experience is explicated. Mathematical nature-knowledge is made the prototype for the foundation, and the social sciences are determined only in contrast with the natural sciences "with reference *to these* through *being-other*."[325]

Whereas in his critique of naturalism Husserl has experimental psychology in mind as the supposed foundational discipline of philosophy, in his *critique of historicism* he orients himself above all against Dilthey. In historicism Husserl rejects an excess of determinate scientific ideas. For him, history [*Geschichte*] is taken only as object of a group of sciences, historiography [*Historie*]. But this deals only with facts. For this reason an excess of the historical as historiographical in

---

323 Ibid., 72.
324 Ibid.
325 Ibid., 83.

the sense of historicism cannot make any contribution to philosophy as rigorous science. Rather, from concrete factual material of psychic-historical life "the manifolds of configurations as shapes of sense"[326] are to be established. "The idea of observing the historical is a morphology or typology of historical happenings," in which "*historical Dasein is totally degraded.*"[327] In Husserl's critique of naturalism as well as of historicism [108] – through preoccupation with known cognition, that is, through the *primary* preoccupation with *securing* an *absolutely certain* knowledge – "*human Dasein as such is excluded from the possibility of being encountered.*"[328] The difference that guides Husserl's observation of the historical, between the factual and the valid, is drawn from theoretical comportment as judgment. But, given this origin, the question arises: By what right dare this difference, thus arisen, be extended to every psychic configuration?

In view of Husserl's clearly outlined idea of philosophy as rigorous science, one must ask above all: Wherein here is *the preoccupation with the thinghood of things themselves*? The preoccupation with known cognition, which is enacted in Husserl's self-interpretation of phenomenology, is preoccupation with "*justified knowledge,*" with the "*most valid knowledge,*" with "*an evident all-binding unity.*"[329] From the very beginning this knowledge is taken as the only scientific knowledge. The goal of this preoccupation is primarily "to create generally any possible, absolutely binding sort of cognition," while "*what* in this cognition is to be known is from the very beginning secondary."[330] For philosophy as rigorous science, *the things themselves* present themselves only under the *assumption* that they fit with the *idea of absolute cognition accepted in advance*. But with that, the phenomenological maxim "to the things themselves" gets lost under a completely defined and *not self-evident* interpretation. Now, in transcendental phenomenology characterized as rigorous science, "to the things themselves" no longer means – as it still did in *Logical Investigations* – "to make things freely present from out of themselves *prior to* a certain way of questioning, but rather it means: to let what is asked about be encountered *within this very determinately*

---

326 Ibid., 93.
327 Ibid.
328 Ibid.
329 Ibid., 101.
330 Ibid.

prescribed   problematic."[331] [109] But at the same time, Heidegger acknowledges again that the phenomenological maxim, even in Husserl's interpretation – which limits the encountering possibility of things themselves – still has "a certain originality over against the constructions of contemporary philosophy."[332] Yet at the same time, it cannot be overlooked that the transcendental-phenomenological interpretation of the maxim "lets lie outside the sphere of vision the much *more fundamental possibility of releasing beings in such a way* that the corresponding worthiness of beings to be asked about decides what is the primary object of philosophy."[333] Regarding this decision it says that it must be released in itself, "towards the possibility that such a knowledge has nothing to do with an idea of science that is taken from mathematics, that such a decidability stemming from releasement of things perhaps first of all enacts the genuine sense of knowledge."[334]

However, Husserl's preoccupation with known cognition does not rest in a formal indifference as regards its being; rather, it is a *factual-historical preoccupation*. As such it exists in the historical tradition of the Cartesian *cogito sum* as the *certum*, which for its part is determined from the preoccupation of known cognition. Husserl takes over the *cogito sum*, and the certitude that belongs to it, as the self-evident starting point for the transcendental and eidetic reduction. But Descartes's philosophy of the *cogito sum* includes the medieval ontology that he obviously takes over. Heidegger's tracing of Husserl's phenomenological critique back to Descartes's ontology of the *cogito sum* is intended to show that Husserl's phenomenology of transcendental consciousness is beset with ontological implications of which Husserl himself is not aware and which therefore belong to the phenomenologically unaccounted-for assumptions of Husserl's phenomenology.

[110]

§ 3. Preoccupation with Certitude and the Deformation of Phenomenological Findings

It is the preoccupation with certitude associated with Descartes that "deforms"[335] the *positive phenomenological findings of Husserl*. Heidegger

---

331   Ibid., 102.
332   Ibid.
333   Ibid.
334   Ibid.
335   Ibid., 270.

treats these *deformations* in three respects: "(1) with respect to *intentionality* itself, (2) with respect to the frame of *evidence*, and (3) with respect to the determination of phenomenological research as *eidetic*."[336] Alongside the categorical intuition, it is the *intentionality* of consciousness that Heidegger counts among the greatest discoveries of Husserlian phenomenology, because of its ground-breaking character. Heidegger designates the structure of intentionality as follows. With the respective *cogitare* the *cogitatum* is given "as what is [*Seiendes*] in the how of its respective encountering for access and handling."[337] Here he says:

> With this discovery of intentionality the way is expressly given, for the first time in the whole history of philosophy, for radical ontological research.[338]

> As long as I do not have this foundation, I am not capable of seeing something like a being-character, in any sense at all of direct observation of beings – and thus of doing anything like ontology.[339]

This positive appreciation clearly shows two things: on the one hand, the way in which Heidegger grabs hold of Husserl's discovery of intentionality for his own phenomenological questioning – and makes it fruitful; and on the other hand, that Husserl precisely did *not* go this way, because of his preoccupation with certitude, which destined him and hindered him. Heidegger sees the deformation of intentionality in this "being grasped, less explicitly than implicitly, always as *specific theoretical* self-comportment,"[340] that is, as a [111] meaning-of-something, which sketches out the direction of the view for every intentional analysis. At the same time, this theoretical meaning forms the foundation of the multi-level intentional ways of consciousness. The study of intentionality is oriented primarily toward what is intentional in *cognizing*. Correspondingly, beings [*das Seiende*] in their intentional being-given are also captured in the *theoretical* apprehension. This is shown by the fact that the real being as *natural thing* forms the foundation for all other being-possibilities, such as culture and history, in which it can be apprehended. The predominance of the theoretical, that

---

336 Ibid.
337 Ibid., 260.
338 Ibid.
339 Ibid., 262.
340 Ibid., 271.

is, perceiving and observing cognition of nature, is driven by the preoccupation with certitude.

Regarding the phenomenological thematization of *evidence*, Heidegger stresses that everything that Husserl has carried out in this regard is far beyond anything previously said in philosophy. This is because, for the first time ever, Husserl has placed evidence on a proper foundation. Yet one sees that Husserl is acquainted only with *"evidence of grasping and determining,"*[341] which is analogously carried over to the other ways of comportment and their evidence. But therein is manifest a deformation of the evidence-phenomenon through the dominant preoccupation with known cognition. For Heidegger "the *actual* question of evidence in the fundamental sense" begins "with the question of the *specific* evidence of access to a being and of disclosing this being."[342] "Evidence has its place only within this phenomenon thus envisaged."[343] Whereas for Husserl phenomenological cognition first becomes valid scientific knowledge when it is essential cognition through the *eidetic reduction*, for Heidegger phenomenological research is deformed precisely through this method. The basic genres, and the kinds of lived-experiences of consciousness subordinate to them, are meant to be gained through eidetic cognition. [112] Eidetic reduction moves in the ontological determinations of genre, kind, specific difference, and eidetic singularity, that is, categories "that have their defined basis and *say nothing about such a being as consciousness.*"[344] With that, through the eidetic reduction, ontological determinations of another source are transferred to consciousness. From here Husserl comes finally to conceive of the idea of a mathematical science [*Mathesis*] of lived-experiences, that is, to determine purely *a priori* the pure possibilities of lived-experiences. Here once again is manifest very clearly how Husserl interprets the phenomenological maxim "to the things themselves." The things themselves are lived-experiences of consciousness, insofar as they are subordinated not only to the transcendental reduction but also to the eidetic one. Within the preoccupation with the known cognition – which is the preoccupation that belongs to Husserl's transcendental phenomenology – it is not possible to come "to

---

341 Ibid., 273.
342 Ibid.
343 Ibid.
344 Ibid., 274.

understand *life itself in its genuine being* and to answer the *question of its being-character.*"[345]

§ 4. Preoccupation with the Disclosure of Dasein Itself

Heidegger's answer to Husserl's Freiburg phenomenology of transcendental consciousness is the *hermeneutic phenomenology of Dasein.* Here we are reminded of Heidegger's own designation of his relationship to Husserl during the years 1918 to 1923, from *Being and Time*:

> If the following investigation takes some steps forward in disclosing the "things themselves," the author thanks first of all E. Husserl, who made the author familiar with the most varied areas of phenomenological research during his teaching years in Freiburg, through compelling personal guidance and through the most liberal bequeathing of unpublished investigations.[346]

[113] And further, at the same place in the text it says: "The following investigations were possible only on the foundation that E. Husserl laid, with whose *Logical Investigations* phenomenology made a breakthrough."[347] The investigation of *Being and Time* goes "some steps forward ... in the disclosing of 'the things themselves,'" in that it – through a *freer self-surrender to the phenomenological maxim* – embraces the *possibility* of the phenomenology of Dasein that is *hidden* in the phenomenology of consciousness. In the end what is presented in *Being and Time* as hermeneutic phenomenology of Dasein begins in 1919 under the name of *pre-theoretical primordial science of living and living-experience* and eventually takes the names *scientific origin of factical life, ontological phenomenology,* and *hermeneutic of facticity.* Just as Husserl in his phenomenology of consciousness strives to lay the foundation for philosophy as a whole, so too does Heidegger, beginning with the war emergency semester of 1919,[348] try to ground anew the idea of philosophy and with that philosophy as a whole, under the title of pre-theoretical primordial

---

345 Ibid., 275.
346 Heidegger, *Sein und Zeit*, GA 2, 52; EA, 38.
347 Ibid., 51f.
348 Heidegger, *Die Idee der Philosophie und das Weltanschaungungsproblem*, in *Zur Bestimmung der Philosophie*, GA 56/57.

science of living and living-experience. This is above all a matter of hermeneutically-phenomenologically revealing living and living-experience in its pre-theoretical character, which has never been seen and determined as such by philosophy, not even by Greek philosophy. When Heidegger also appeals to the phenomenological method of returning to the things themselves, for gaining access to pre-theoretical life, this is precisely where he introduces his critique of Husserl, who oriented phenomenology and thus its principle in terms of the priority of the theoretical. This predominance of theoretical cognizing and thinking, which goes back all the way to Greek philosophy, is what – in the philosophical handling of soul, life, or spirit – never led to life's being able to be encountered freely from itself, that is, without the leap ahead into the theoretical. In that [114] this leap ahead is seen as a *preconception that is not grounded within the things themselves*, and in that life itself is prevented from showing itself in its ownmost being-character, a dimension of things opens up that has remained hidden up to now, within which philosophy experiences the laying of a new foundation. In this sense the first Marburg lecture course says:

> But now, insofar as the outstanding situation for us consists in the fact that, through the dominance of the preoccupation of science-education, all areas of life and being-worlds are theoretized in an idiosyncratic manner, the fundamental task arises of first of all going back behind this theorizing, in order to *gain anew the possible starting position from within Dasein itself.*[349]

The priority of the theoretical in the interpretation of living and living-experience belongs to the essential determination of human being as rational creature, to which Husserl specifically appeals once again in his last major work, *The Crisis of the European Sciences and Transcendental Phenomenology*.[350] In traditional philosophy this essential determination forms the explicit or implicit guide for all philosophical questions. Husserl's interpretation of the phenomenological maxim "to the things themselves" is likewise determined through that guide. If Heidegger sees the predominance of the theoretical as the preconception of both traditional philosophy and Husserl's interpretation of phenomenology,

---

349 Heidegger, *Einführung in die phänomenologische Forschung*, GA 17, 269.
350 Husserl, *Die Krisis der europäischen Wissenschaften und die transzendentale Phänomenologie*, in *Huss.*, VI, 13; ET, 8.

then a-theoretical life, or Dasein, takes the place of the previous philosophical guide, as the new and future guide of philosophy. Hermeneutic phenomenology of pre-theoretical Dasein in *Being and Time* is the *working out of a new guide for philosophy*. In its every step this working out follows the phenomenological principle "to the things themselves," liberated from the predominance of the theoretical. In this explicitly phenomenological way of seeing and [115] letting Dasein be encountered from within itself, in an unencumbered fashion, the analyses in the interpretation must also be taken into account. Transcendence and horizon in their belonging-together form the basic structure of Dasein. In the transition to being-historical enowning-thinking, Heidegger breaks with this transcendental-horizonal structure of Dasein but not the hermeneutic-phenomenological insights into the ways of being and the being-characteristics of Dasein. For, as thrown and by that means now enowned throwing-open, Dasein is located in enowning. But the experience of the historicality of being and of the belonging-together of being and Dasein as enowning remains determined through what is unique in phenomenology, which is expressed in the call "to the things themselves." For when being-historical thinking is determined as such, as that which thinks not "about" being, but rather "from within" being itself – namely, always that which shows itself in the enowning throw as what is to be taken up into the thinking throwing open – then enowning-thinking knows itself to be bound only "to the things themselves."

Heidegger's deciding answer to Husserl's Freiburg phenomenology lies in the *lack of reservation* with which he follows the call of the fundamental principle of phenomenology as formulated by Husserl: "to the things themselves." His critique of Husserlian phenomenology is an utterly *phenomenological* critique, one that arises from the *more radical* grasping of the phenomenological maxim. When taken seriously, what is radical about this maxim is its central phenomenological insight that what is primary in phenomenological philosophy dare not be a preconceived idea of scientific knowledge. Rather, what is *primary* is that *things are able to freely present themselves*, which first traces out the character of scientificality. What Heidegger, for his own phenomenological approach, owes to Husserl, he says in the preface to the last of his early Freiburg lecture courses, *Ontology – The Hermeneutics of Facticity*, in an unsurpassable manner: "*Husserl* gave me eyes to see."[351]

---

351 Heidegger, *Ontologie (Hermeneutik der Faktizität)*, GA 63, 5.

Part Three

Hermeneutic Phenomenology of Dasein and Reflective Phenomenology of Consciousness

[119]

§ 1. Hermeneutic Phenomenology in *Being and Time*

The launching of *hermeneutic* phenomenology in the war emergency semester lecture course happened from within a *thematic-methodological primordial experience*. Thematically it was the primordial experience of a-theoretical life and living-experience – which simultaneously included the methodological primordial experience – that access to the realm of the a-theoretical cannot be reflection, but rather only hermeneutics, which must first be cultivated. Linked to this thematic-methodological primordial experience is the fundamental insight that a-theoretical life – and correlatively, the a-theoretical life-world – is not a grounding-interconnection, in which sense experience and the sensorily experienced corporeal world is what grounds all higher-level life of consciousness. Thus, what belongs to the thematic-methodological primordial experience is the trailblazing insight that the thought of such a grounding-interconnection is not drawn phenomenologically from out of a-theoretical life, but rather arises from the reflective-theoretical access to life and the life of consciousness.

This thematic and methodological primordial experience and insight is what stands out in the hermeneutics founded by Heidegger. Methodologically and thematically, all of the early Freiburg and Marburg lecture courses from the war emergency onward are governed by the hermeneutic primordial experience. Thus all methodological elaborations in these lecture texts must always be read within the horizon of the hermeneutic primordial experience. The stream of hermeneutic phenomenology of the a-theoretical, of factical life – begun with the war emergency semester – flows into the systematically worked out hermeneutic phenomenology of *Being and Time*. In § 7 of the Introduction, the section of that work on methodology, Heidegger unfolds his "anticipatory grasp" of the hermeneutic phenomenology of Dasein. Insofar as the hermeneutic of Dasein is *phenomenology*, it takes up the methodological idea of phenomenology that was established by Husserl, expressed in the principle of all [120] principles and in the research-maxim "returning to the things themselves." But to the extent that phenomenology of Dasein is *hermeneutics*, it is differentiated from Husserl's phenomenology, which holds sway in the acts of reflection. The section of *Being and Time* on methodology is to be understood in its deepest intentions only from within a connection with and countering of Husserl's reflective phenomenology. Without a fundamental knowledge of Husserlian phenomenology in the methodological and thematic sense, a reading of the section on methodology must remain blunted. The connection to the phenomenological research-maxim, as well as the countering of the key reflective feature of Husserlian phenomenology, form the background against which Heidegger unfolds the anticipatory grasp of hermeneutic phenomenology. It is true that Heidegger explicitly mentions Husserl only toward the end of the section on methodology, but he does so in a way that calls the reader to listen attentively. For that section demonstrates how hermeneutic phenomenology of Dasein was possible only from out of the encounter with reflective phenomenology of consciousness. Therefore it is by thinking through the elaborations of the section on methodology with a view to Husserl's phenomenology that we recognize where Heidegger joins with this and where he distances himself from it. But that means we must also delineate the key features of Husserl's concept of reflective phenomenology of consciousness.

The unique feature in the unfolding of the anticipatory grasp of hermeneutic phenomenology in the section of *Being and Time* on methodology consists in the fact that here the hermeneutic-phenomenological method is portrayed according to its *two principles* of way of treatment and method of access. In the methodological principle of way of treatment, Husserl's established phenomenological research-maxim "returning to the things themselves" is taken up. The second principle, of method of access, formulates the directives for methodological access to the hermeneutic field of investigation. The hermeneutic-phenomenological method of access consists of the three-fold directives that are own to opening, access, and passage-through; in the revised working-out [121] of the third section of the first part of *Being and Time* – "Time and Being" – these are clarified as herme-neutic reduction, hermeneutic construction, and hermeneutic destruc-tion. Husserl's reflective-phenomenological method is also structured according to two principles; the first expresses the phenomenological research-maxim, and thus the way of treatment, whereas the second is a method of access, the reflective-phenomenological epoché and re-duction. Accordingly, in the second and third sections of this essay, we think through both of the methodological principles – for hermeneu-tic phenomenology and for reflective phenomenology – and compare them with each other. In the final section we turn our attention to the fundamental determination of hermeneutics from out of the section on methodology, the aim of which can only be understood if it is viewed in its demarcation from phenomenological reflection. If the *logos* of phe-nomenology is a hermeneutic one, then the phenomenological way of treatment and the method of access that belongs to it are of a hermeneu-tic nature. If, however, the *logos* of phenomenology is determined re-flectively, then the phenomenological way of treatment and the method of access have a reflective character.

Here, too, in contrasting the concepts of hermeneutic and reflective phenomenology , our concern is to demonstrate both ways of phenom-enology; even when they are set against each other in total acuity, each one bears its own truth.

[122]

§ 2. Phenomenology as Way of Treatment (First Methodological Principle)

(a) The Formal Concept of Phenomenology in Husserl and in Heidegger

At the beginning of the section on methodology,[352] Heidegger empha-sizes that phenomenology is primarily a *concept of method*, which does not name the thematic object of philosophy, but rather the *how* of its

---

352 Heidegger, *Sein und Zeit*, GA 2, 37; EA, 27.

investigation, the way of treatment. In connection with Husserl's text, we are all too easily inclined to equate the title "phenomenology" with the intentional analysis of lived-experiences of consciousness; in connection with Heidegger's text, with the existential analysis of Dasein. In such equating we do not pay enough heed to the fact that phenomenology means *primarily*, not the thematic object and not the "material what of objects of philosophical research,"[353] but rather its *way* of investigation. Phenomenology is not a philosophical discipline alongside ontology, epistemology, or ethics, because as *method* it does not have its own thematic subject area alongside the subject areas of ontology, epistemology, or ethics. Each of these disciplines could be designated as phenomenology, that is, if it wanted to be understood phenomenologically in the *methodic* sense. The intentional composition of acts of consciousness is not what actually makes up the phenomenological in phenomenology of consciousness; rather, what is phenomenological here is the specific *method* with the help of which philosophical reflection discovers the intentional composition. And in the same way, the existential structures, which make up the being (existence) of Dasein as a structural whole, are not what *actually* make up the phenomenological in the phenomenology of Dasein; rather, what is phenomenological here too is the *method* that has led to the analytic release of the structures of human being.

[123] The thematic object of *Being and Time* – the being of beings and the sense of being in general – is to be handled *phenomenologically*. Because phenomenology is primarily a methodological concept, "this treatise is committed neither to a 'standpoint' nor to a 'direction,' because phenomenology is neither of these and can never be such, as long as it knows itself clearly."[354] Heidegger's emphasis on phenomenology's *independence of standpoint* and *freedom from direction* is one of those formulations that he intentionally keeps ambiguous. Heidegger highlights the words *standpoint* and *direction* because with them he is referring back to Husserl. In Husserl these words belong to that context where he expresses the self-understanding of the phenomenological method. The first "tone" in which Heidegger's repudiation of a standpoint and a direction attempts to be heard is his positive embrace of Husserl's self-understanding about the phenomenological method. In

---

353 Ibid.
354 Ibid.

the introduction to volume II of *Logical Investigations*, Husserl formulates the phenomenological method's freedom from standpoint and direction as *the principle of lack of presupposition*.[355] In the first book of *Ideas Pertaining to a Pure Phenomenology and to a Phenomenological Philosophy* he describes the characteristic, basic attitude of phenomenology as follows: we take "our starting point from that which lies *prior to* all standpoint: from the whole region of what is given intuitively and still before any theoretical thinking, from all of that which one can see and grasp immediately."[356] A few pages before that[357] he speaks of the "factical philosophical directions" for which philosophy that works phenomenologically has no use.

[124] We can gather together what Husserl understands by independence of standpoint and freedom from direction in philosophy that proceeds phenomenologically, as follows: Phenomenological philosophy is to be grounded as scientific philosophy by explicitly setting aside predetermined standpoints and directions. In its starting point and in its execution as nascent philosophical science, its intention is to reject predetermined standpoints and directions. In this sense it intends to establish its philosophical findings without presuppositions – to establish them only in psychic-reflective looking at what is given intuitively to the reflective-gazing look and what can be psychically seen and grasped as intuitively given.

When Heidegger says that *Being and Time* is not dedicated to any standpoint or any direction and that the thematic object of his treatise is treated *phenomenologically*, he is identifying initially with Husserl's characterization of phenomenology. For Heidegger as for Husserl, "phenomenology" is not a standpoint shaped by content, nor is it a direction determined by content; rather, it is a methods-concept. As such, phenomenology for Husserl as well does not mean the thematic object of philosophy, but rather the *how* of its *treatment*.

But Heidegger's emphasis on freedom from standpoint and from direction is to be heard simultaneously in a second "tone," in which his methodological and thematic independence – over against Husserl – gets expressed. In this second tone he declares to the reader that *Being and Time*, proceeding phenomenologically, is not dedicated somehow

355 Husserl, *Logische Untersuchungen*, II/1, 9; *Huss.*, XIX/1, 24; ET, I, 262.
356 Husserl, *Ideen* …, 38; *Huss.*, III, 46.
357 Ibid., 33 (*Huss.*, III, 41).

to Husserlian phenomenology either methodologically or thematically. The first tone is not "nullified" by the second; the second does not set itself against the first but rather intensifies it. In the second tone Heidegger is taking Husserl at his word: if phenomenology as methodological concept is independent of content-related philosophical standpoints and directions, then it must *also be independent* of the *specific expression* that Husserl has given to the phenomenological method [125] and be independent of the thematic region that Husserl has determined to be *the* object of phenomenological philosophy. It is true that Husserl practised the phenomenological method of reflectively-gazing grasping – that is, of what is brought to intuitive givenness therein, for the most part in freedom from standpoint and from direction. However, what he thematized as the field of investigation of phenomenological philosophy, and what he recognized as such with the help of the phenomenological method – namely, the egoical life of consciousness with its intentionally composed lived-experiences – this appeared henceforth as the unquestioned object of phenomenological philosophy. With that, phenomenology itself became in retrospect a methodologically and thematically established standpoint. Phenomenology as method became at the same time a thematically and firmly shaped philosophy: at first phenomenology of lived-experiences of pure consciousness, then phenomenology of lived-experience of transcendental consciousness, namely, transcendental subjectivity. If Heidegger in *Being and Time* invokes the phenomenological method first established by Husserl (first tone), he then must simultaneously have the reader understand that he is thereby committed neither to the phenomenological standpoint that Husserl has put into practice nor to any other predefined phenomenological direction, for example, that of Max Scheler (second tone). Just as Husserl, in the name of phenomenology as method and for his phenomenological research, demands independence from traditional standpoints and directions, so does Heidegger *in the same terms* demand independence from the predetermined phenomenological reality. It is in this sense that Heidegger says, toward the end of the section on methodology, that what is essential to phenomenology does not lie in "being *actual* as a philosophical 'direction.' Higher than actuality is *possibility*. The understanding of phenomenology lies solely in embracing it as possibility."[358]

---

358 Heidegger, *Sein und Zeit*, GA 2, 51f.; EA, 38.

Just as Husserl plied the phenomenological method as methodological independence over against existing standpoints and directions, [126] so too does Heidegger mean to enact phenomenological seeing independently of the prescribed phenomenological directions.

This characterization of phenomenology as methods-concept, by stressing freedom from standpoint and from direction, is however only a *negative* description, which as such requires a *positive* designation of the phenomenological method. This positive aspect does indeed come through in the negative description; but it is really set into motion when phenomenology is formulated through its research-maxim: "To the things themselves!" Heidegger sets this maxim in quotation marks[359] because he wants to refer to Husserl with it. In the introduction to volume II of *Logical Investigations*, quoted earlier, we read: "We want to go back to 'the things themselves.' With fully developed intuitions we want to bring before us the evidence that what is given here in actually enacted abstraction is truly and actually that which the word-meanings in the lawful expression mean {meant here are the ideal laws of pure logic}."[360] And in *Ideas I* Husserl says: "To judge rationally and scientifically about things means to orient oneself to the *things themselves*, that is, to return from the discourses and meanings to the things themselves, to inquire of them in their self-givenness and to set aside all preconceptions that are foreign to the things."[361]

In the quotation from *Logical Investigations*, besides the phrase "going back to the things themselves," the term *evidence* appears. These belong together. In the reflective-gazing look to the thing (the respective thematic object of philosophizing), bringing this to intuitive givenness, just as it is in itself – this means nothing other than bringing it in reflective gazing to evidence for oneself. We dare not translate "evidence" in Husserl merely as "certitude." Husserl uses this word in its literal meaning of looking-out-from and [127] of insight in the sense of reflective gazing and what is gazed at therein. In *Ideas I* Husserl also designates the phenomenological method that underlies the maxim "to the things themselves!" as the *principle of all principles*;[362] and in the *Cartesian Meditations* he designates it as the *principle of evidence* and defines

359 Ibid., 37; EA, 27.
360 Husserl, *Logische Untersuchungen*, II/1, 6; *Huss.*, XIX/1, 10; ET, 252.
361 Husserl, *Ideen I*, 35; *Huss.*, III, 42.
362 Ibid., 43; *Huss.*, III, 52.

it as the *first methodological principle*,[363] which as first calls for at least a second.

For Husserl this first principle of the phenomenological method says that I in the course of my philosophizing investigation "dare not make any judgment or let anything be valid that I have not drawn from evidence, from *experiences* in which the things in question and the complex of things are present to me *as* they themselves."[364] Husserl comprehends evidence as a setting-eyes-psychically-on-the-thing-itself.[365]

When Heidegger in his explanation of the phenomenological method emphasizes freedom from standpoint and from direction and refers to the maxim "to the things themselves!", he positively embraces *only* what is for Husserl the first methodological principle, the principle of evidence still understood formally, which Husserl grasps as a looking-at-the-thing-itself and which in this formal version is not yet concretized with reference to the distinction between adequate and apodictic evidence. Beyond that, Heidegger takes up this methodological principle of return to the things themselves only in the formal capacity of a *purely methodological concept*, without the Husserlian thematic implication.

However, he does not embrace even this formal methodological concept in the version and formulation that Husserl gave to it. Rather, he develops his *own formal concept of phenomenology*, one that aligns with Husserl's formal evidence-principle only in what is formally and in principle.

But what is *sought after* in the section on methodology is not only the formal [128] concept of phenomenology, but also and above all the *phenomenological* concept of phenomenology.[366] Heidegger means by this the *philosophically concrete* concept of phenomenology – concrete because it is *de*formalized with reference to what the thematic object of a phenomenological method of philosophy is. Besides the phenomenological concept of phenomenology, Heidegger names the *prevalent* one, under which he understands the *positivist-scientific* concept of phenomenology. This too is a concrete concept of phenomenology, insofar as the formal concept of phenomenology has been *de*formalized in it, with reference to what in positive science is an object of research that

---

363 Husserl, *Cartesianische Meditationen und Pariser Vorträge*, 54.
364 Ibid.
365 Ibid., 52.
366 Heidegger, *Sein und Zeit*, GA 2, 42; EA, 31.

is understood as phenomenological. We will see that what is *common* [*gemeinsam*] in the understanding of phenomenology of Heidegger and Husserl is contained in what Heidegger emphasizes as the *formal concept of phenomenology*. Their difference emerges when the question arises regarding the formal concept of phenomenology for Heidegger on the one hand and for Husserl on the other.

The approach that Heidegger pursues for attaining his formal concept of phenomenology proceeds from clarifying the Greek etymology of both parts of the word *phenomen-ology*.[367] Heidegger translates the word *phenomenon*, the Greek φαινόμενον, as "what shows itself in itself and in this sense what is manifest." He does not merely say lexically "self-showing," but rather what shows itself *in itself*, in order to make clear that what shows itself, the self-showing thing, shows itself in the way it is *itself*: how it is *in itself*. Therein is contained this: what the thing shows itself is what the thing *in truth* is.

Heidegger clarifies this formal concept of phenomenology through a twofold dissociation: on the one hand, against the privative modification in the shape of *semblance* [*Schein*],[368] and on the other hand, against what he calls [129] *appearance* [*Erscheinung*].[369] What shows itself just as [*so wie*] it is itself also has the possibility of showing itself in the way that it is *not*. In such a case we say: the thing only looks that way [*so wie*], but in truth it is not so. But by being able to look this way or that way [*so wie*], it must be able to *show itself generally*. Although the Greek word φαινόμενον includes both meanings lexically – as what-shows-itself-in-itself and as the seeming – Heidegger allocates the word *phenomenon* terminologically only for the positive mode of self-showing and grasps the second meaning – the negative one as the privative mode – terminologically as semblance.

Heidegger fully and sharply distinguishes that which he designates terminologically as *appearance* [*Erscheinung*] from phenomenon as what-shows-itself-in-itself and from semblance as what-does-not-show-itself-in-itself. Whereas semblance is a privative modification of self-showing, appearance is not at all self-showing, but rather is only a

---

367 Ibid., 38; EA, 28.
368 Ibid., 38f.; EA, 28f. [Translator's note: As we will see in this paragraph, Heidegger is naming that aspect of the phenomenon that is a seeming/*scheinen*, that is, a semblance/*Schein*.]
369 Ibid., 39ff.; EA, 29f.

presenting. As an example of an appearance over against a self-showing, Heidegger points to what we understand by symptoms of illness – for example, reddened cheeks, which indicate the presence of a fever, which in turn indicates a disturbance in the organism. In the redness of the cheeks the illness *does not show* itself, but rather only *presents itself* – and indeed, it does so *through* the redness of the cheeks, which for its part shows itself. In that the redness shows itself, it *presents* in its self-showing the self-presenting illness, but not as the self-showing of the redness of the cheeks. Heidegger clarifies the profound difference between the phenomenon as what-shows-itself-in-itself and the appearance as a presenting. The latter is not only, like semblance, a privative mode of self-showing but also not a self-showing at all. He clarifies this difference by grasping phenomenon as a distinctive *way of encountering* something, whereas appearance is not a way of encountering, but rather an *entity-based referral-relation* in the entity itself.[370]

[130] As long as it remains unclear what that is that is given in the unique way of encountering the phenomenon, what-shows-itself-in-itself, it is a matter of the *formal concept of phenomenology*.[371]

Designation of what the λόγος in phenomen-*ology* means also belongs to the determination of the formal concept of phenomenology. Heidegger names *discourse* [*die Rede*] as the basic meaning of λόγος, and he cites as the essential character of discourse the *making-manifest* of something, the *showing letting-be-seen*.[372]

If phenomenon means what-shows-itself-in-itself and logos means the showing letting-be-seen, then phenomenology says to the same extent: showing letting-be-seen of what-shows-itself-in-itself. Or, as Heidegger says: "To let that which shows itself be seen from itself, in the very way in which it shows itself from itself."[373] This is Heidegger's version of the formal concept of phenomenology, of which he says that in it the phenomenological research-maxim "to the things themselves!" is expressed. Expressed in this way, the formal concept of phenomenology says: pronounce the issue at stake as truly known only insofar as in a thinking gazing it is *brought* to self-showing-in-itself.

---

370 Ibid., 41; EA, 31.
371 Ibid., 42; EA, 31.
372 Ibid., 43f.; EA, 32.
373 Ibid., 46; EA, 34.

Whatever thematic object is being considered, in every case this object is to encounter scientific treatment and to offer itself in the mode of self-showing-in-itself, so that the scientific treatment can let its object be seen just as it shows itself from it itself and also let itself [the scientific handling] be seen from out of itself – both without falsification. "Phenomenon" does not mean the thematic object itself, but rather only its way of encountering and its mode of self-offering for the investigation; the logos of phenomenology says *how* the thematic object, which encounters in the mode of self-showing-in-itself, is to be *investigated*. The logos of phenomenology – the letting-be-seen-from-itself – takes place, as Heidegger emphasizes, as *direct showing* and *direct revealing*, that is, as showing and revealing immediately in [131] what-shows-itself-in-itself.[374] "Showing" and "revealing" are also basic methodological principles for Husserl, and they belong in the circle of the first methodological principle of formal evidence, about which we have in the meantime learned that in its formal range it is congruent with the formal concept of phenomenology that Heidegger has established.

(b) The Deformalization of the Formal Concept of Phenomenology to the Ordinary (Positivist-Scientific) Concept of Phenomenology

Let us now take up again the anticipatory look – given earlier in our considerations – at the problem of deformalization of the formal concept of phenomenology. This is the problem of the *reference of method to its object*, without thereby cancelling again the divorce between method and thematic object. Deformalization is, as concretization, the question of the content-related determination of the thematic object, which is to be scientifically shown and grasped in the way of encountering self-showing-in-itself.

For Heidegger such a deformalization can basically go in *two directions*. The distinction between these two directions of a concretizing of the formal concept of phenomenology is determined from the fundamental thought of his thematic philosophy – that is, from within the ontological difference between being and beings. Because the question of deformalization is the question of the thematic object in the mode of self-showing-in-itself, deformalization has above all to do with the

---

374 Ibid., 46: EA, 35.

formal concept of *phenomenon*, mindful of the fact that phenomenon is the way of encountering and the mode of self-offering of the thematic object.

The *one* direction in which the formal concept of phenomenology can be concretized is in the direction of *beings*. Beings ... that is simply the sum total of things in the broad sense, non-human beings. Here belong the non-living [132] things of nature, the non-human living beings, the things of use produced by humans, and also the things of art that have been created by humans, what we call artworks. But humans, too, belong among beings, as well as all of the cultivated forms of community and their institutions. Now, if that which is brought to givenness in the mode of self-showing-in-itself is *beings* in whatever region, then the formal concept of phenomenology has been deformalized to the *ordinary* concept of phenomenology. The ordinary concept of phenomenology in its ordinariness refers to an extraordinary concept of phenomenology.

It is important to keep in mind that the ordinary concept of phenomenology does not mean beings as they show themselves in the *pre-scientific* access to them, but rather beings as they are a thematic object of scientific, to wit *positivist-scientific*, research. That becomes clear when Heidegger says that "every showing of beings as they show themselves in themselves" can be called "phenomenology."[375] Every showing of beings – with that is not meant the natural, pre- and outside-scientific access to them, but rather the positivist-scientific access to beings of a scientific research-area. For phenomenology is, in every case and so also as ordinary phenomenology, a *method*, but essentially a scientific one and never the natural way of access. We must differentiate the non-scientific-natural ways of access to that which is, from scientific ways of access.

Of course it is a question proper to philosophy as to what the pre-scientific ways of access are, a question that is to be grasped in a philosophical reflection on them. According to his basic approach, Husserl comprehends the pre- and outside-scientific ways of access as those which he in summary calls simple sense experience (also life-world experience): the present-related and making present perception and its presentiating modifications of the present-related memory of the present, the [133] past-related recollection, and the future-related anticipation (expectation). In contrast, Heidegger, on the basis of his Dasein-approach, calls for, as pre-scientific ways of access, that which

---

375 Ibid., 47; EA, 35.

he designates terminologically as comportments of circumspect caring-for – of the caring dealing with beings near which we always reside.

In pre-scientific everyday life there is no need for a method or methodological showing, in order to bring the things in our natural-everyday life-praxis first and foremost to self-showing. On the other hand, a positivist-scientific investigation of a natural-scientific or humanistic type always needs a method. For it does not want to grasp what always already encounters and is given to us without method; rather, it wants to investigate a region of beings in those respects in which this region does not also already show itself for natural ways of access. The ordinary concepts of phenomenon and of phenomenology say that every positivist-scientific research can be designated as phenomenological in its *method* at that point when, in compliance with its special thing-related and thing-grounded research-methods, it puts itself under the general maxim of grasping that which it wants to know by way of showing and revealing.

(c) The Deformalization of the Formal Concept of Phenomenology to the Phenomenological (Philosophical) Concept of Phenomenology

That was the first of the two directions in which a deformalization of the formal concept of phenomenology can take place. With this direction, one deals with the phenomenological method of the positive sciences and thus not yet with the phenomenological method of philosophy. But the section of *Being and Time* on methodology deals exclusively with the determination of *phenomenology as method of philosophy*. The thematic object of philosophy for Heidegger is the *being* of beings, and specifically in such a way that the question of the being of beings is carried by the question of [134] the sense of being in general. If the formal concept of phenomenology is deformalized in the direction of the being of beings and their sense, then we attain the *philosophical*, the *proper*, and thus the *phenomenological* phenomenon- and phenomenology-concept.

(α) Heidegger's Deformalization of the Formal Concept of Phenomenon in the Direction of the Being of Beings: Self-Related-Ecstatic-Horizonal Disclosure of Being

In response to the fact that the formal concept of phenomenology must be deformalized to the philosophical-phenomenological concept of phenomenology, in the direction of the *being* of beings, Heidegger turns to four interwoven questions.[376] In an unspoken preview of the matter

[*Sachheit*] of the being of beings, these questions should give insight into how far *being* and not beings is the showing and revealing phenomenon in the strict sense, and that means in the phenomenological sense.

The *first* question asks: with reference to what must the formal concept of phenomenology, what-shows-itself-in-itself, be deformalized to the phenomenological and how does the phenomenological differ from the ordinary? The *second* question asks: What object is phenomenology as method of philosophy, phenomenological philosophy, to let be seen? *Letting*-be-seen comprises the fact that through it the object, the thing, is first of all shown and *brought* to the self-showing-in-itself. But that is also true – as we saw – of that which the positive sciences always demonstrate with their research-object. Therefore, that which phenomenology as method of philosophy is to let be seen must be something that is *not* shown in the natural and pre-scientific encounter of beings but also not in the scientific thematization of beings – something that positive science can never let be seen, but rather only philosophy [135] can – something that only philosophy can demonstrate and bring to self-showing. Thus the *third* question watches out for what can be named *phenomenon* in an "unique" and not an ordinary sense. With that, already in the form of the question, it is said that what is unique in what-shows-itself-in-itself are neither the natural nor the positivist-scientific self-showing beings. The *fourth* question sharpens the third: "What is in its essence *necessarily* the theme of an *explicit* showing?"[377] Which thing on the basis of its thinghood is necessarily the thematic object of an *explicit* showing? "Explicit" is set in italics because here it is a matter of an explicit showing of a unique kind over against that of the positive sciences. Manifestly, there is need for an *explicit* showing because, in showing, phenomenology is to allow to be seen that which does not show itself in either the natural or the positivist-scientific access to beings. All four questions intend step by step to open the view for a matter that, because it does not show itself for either the natural or the positivist-scientific access to beings, demands – *necessarily from it itself* as the only appropriate way of treatment of its thematic investigation – the phenomenological method as explicit showing.

---

376 Ibid.
377 Ibid.

The third and fourth questions have already prepared the *answer*, so that it needs only be expressed. The answer follows in such a way that before he gives a name to *what* phenomenology is to let be seen, Heidegger characterizes this "what" formally, namely, in its relationship to the self-showing of the natural as well as to the positivist-scientific access. The decisive answer reads: "Manifestly it is something that at first and foremost does *not* show itself at all, something that over against what shows itself first and foremost is *hidden*, but at the same time is something that belongs essentially to that which first and foremost shows itself, so much so that it constitutes its [that which shows itself] sense and ground."[378] The thing, which on the basis of its thinghood requires an explicit showing in the eminent sense, so that it can become phenomenon, a self-showing-itself-in-itself [136] – this thing is a thing that "first and foremost does *not* show itself at all," neither in the natural nor in the positivist-scientific self-showing of beings. As a thing that does *not* show itself, it is *hidden*, over against the beings that show themselves outside-science and in positive science. The "not" and the "hidden" are written in italics. What is stressed in the italicized "*not*" indicates that the what of phenomenology cannot be found in and among beings. To stress the "being-hidden" of the what of phenomenology is to point to the fact that the hiddenness of the what of phenomenology is not accidental to it, but rather belongs essentially to it and co-constitutes the thinghood of this thing of phenomenology that is own to it. Since hiddenness belongs essentially to the thinghood of this thing, it is this thing that is to be uncovered from this hiddenness, in a unique letting-be-seen. Only as a thing so *uncovered* in the phenomenological-showing letting-be-seen is it phenomenon, a something-that-shows-itself-in-itself. Yet the hidden thing of phenomenology in the natural and positive-scientific self-showing is *not disconnected* from the natural and positivist-scientific self-showing of beings. Rather they are connected in a distinctive way. As a thing so hidden, it is something that *belongs* "essentially" *to* what is outside the scientific as well as positivist-scientific self-showing of beings. The manner of *how* the hidden thing belongs to the self-showing of beings Heidegger specifies as "its sense and ground." That means: The outside-the-scientific self-showing of beings, which does not need a *methodological* showing,

---

378 Ibid.

and the positivist-scientific, methodologically determined self-showing of beings *are grounded* in the hidden thing.

Now, as to what sense and ground of all self-showing of beings is, Heidegger tells us at the beginning of the following paragraph: "But what remains *hidden* in an exceptional sense or falls back again into *hiding* or shows itself only 'disguised,' is not this or that being, but rather – as the previous observations [137] have shown – the *being* of beings."[379] The sense and ground in which beings with their self-showing are grounded, is the *being* of beings. The appellation "sense" reminds us of Heidegger's formulation of his basic question of the sense of being in general.

In order to get an overall, if still necessarily formal, understanding of *what* the *being* of beings is, in its difference from beings and *how* it is *sense* and *ground* of beings and their self-showing, we turn to two sentences from section 2 of *Being and Time*, where Heidegger offers an initial and directive formal indication of what being is in *difference* from and in its *relation* to beings. These sentences should serve as a guide for our outlining characterization of what in phenomenology is to become phenomenon in a distinctive sense. The first sentence reads: "In the question to be worked out, *what is asked about* is being, that which determines beings as beings, that on the basis of which beings are always already understood, however they may be discussed."[380] That means that, in its relation to beings, being is that which lets beings *be* as beings and *show themselves* as beings; as such, it is however *at the same time* that *on the basis of which* we have in advance ("always already") understood beings, whenever we comport ourselves to them outside of science as well as in scientific research.

But within being Heidegger distinguishes manifold ways of being: the ownmost and unique way of being of beings that we ourselves are, *existence*, as well as ways of being of non-human beings – such as being-ready-to-hand, being-present-at-hand – life, standing-reserve [*Bestand*] (the last one as the way of being of mathematical objects). In the context of our project, it is enough now if we limit ourselves to the ways of being of non-human beings and then specifically to the ways of being of *being-ready-to-hand*. This appellation names the way of being of that being with whom we deal, are engaged, and go around, every day in

---

379 Ibid.
380 Ibid., 8; EA, 6.

the various areas of our private and public social intercourse. The ways of dealing-with, being-engaged-with, [138] and going-around-with, and all other modes of our everyday dealings are what Heidegger comprehends as *the comportments of circumspective concern*. Being-ready-to-hand is the ownmost way of being of that which we also call things of use in a very broad sense. Now, if being is that which determines beings as beings, then being as being-ready-to-hand is that which determines beings as ready-to-hand beings, as beings-ready-to-hand. The ready-to-hand thing of use is only what it is in its difference from a present-at-hand thing of nature, on the basis of its being-ready-to-hand. But *at the same time* being-ready-to-hand is that on the basis of which we, in our daily involvement with the beings that are ready-to-hand, understand this being in advance as a thing of use that is ready-to-hand in this way or that. We must have understood the being-ready-to-hand in advance, so that we can comport ourselves understandingly to the things of use in our private and public surrounding world. In a word: My comporting myself to beings in understanding is already held in a preceding understanding of the being of this being, from which I always already understand the being for the enactment of my comportment to it.

However, being is not only that to which I comport myself, but I myself am also one who comport myself to ready-to-hand beings. The way of being that is own to me is *existence*. In section 4, Heidegger gives the formal indication of existence. I, who comport myself essentially to other beings, am not a being that just "happens among other beings"; rather, I am the being for whom "this being itself is an *issue*."[381] That for me in my being, my being is an *issue* means that I comport myself in my being *to* my being. As way of being, existence is a *relationship-with-being*.[382] In my being I comport myself to my being, insofar as I *understand myself in my being*.[383] The relationship-to-being of my being is the way of my understanding of being, the way in which I understand my own being.

The formal indication for being in its relation to beings (cf. § 2 of *Being and Time*), which up to now we have elucidated only with reference to [139] non-human beings to which I comport myself, also includes being as *existence* in its relation to existing beings. Then existence is also

---

381 Ibid., 16; EA, 12.
382 Ibid.
383 Ibid.

that which *determines* me as the being that I am in each case for me my-self and at the same time that *on the basis of which* I have always already *understood* myself as the being that I myself am. In my comportment to ready-to-hand beings, I also conduct myself always toward myself – even if not in the way in which I conduct myself to ready-to-hand be-ings, still in the ways in which I carry myself in my activities. But in or-der to be able, in my comportments to beings ready-to-hand, to conduct myself to me myself as a being and therein to be able to understand *me myself as a being*, I need preceding guidance through an *understanding of my own being* as existence. For only insofar as my being involves me in my being, only insofar as I understand myself in my being, can I conduct myself to me as a being, as the being that I am for me myself in my activities, that is, understand myself as the being that I am in my activities. As we, in the face of the ready-to-hand being, that is, the non-human being, differentiate between it and its being, in the same way we differentiate with regard to ourselves. The question of the reference by which I myself am a being in its difference from my being – this ques-tion has already been answered. We need only formulate the answer once more explicitly. I am *a being* for me myself in the way of my com-portments to beings that I myself am not. In these comportments I exist *corporeally*. My comportments as a being, my ontic comportments, are constituted corporeally, are ways in which I corporeally deal with and go around with the ready-to-hand. The corporeality of my comport-ments belongs to the way in which I am an existing *being*, on the basis of my being as existence.

In summary, it is a matter of heeding a coupling in the comport-ment to beings as well as in understanding the being of beings. I al-ways conduct myself to non-human beings, and in these comportments I also and essentially conduct myself to myself as a being. My ontic self-comportment is previously illuminated and enabled through my understanding of my own being as existence; my ontic comportment to ready-to-hand beings [140] is previously illuminated and enabled through my understanding of being-ready-to-hand.

To that first formal indication of being in its relation to beings be-longs the second sentence: "The being of beings 'is' not itself a be-ing."[384] That is the first formal indication for the basic thought of the *ontological difference*. In the meantime we have come to know being in

---

384 Ibid., 8; EA, 6.

both modifications of being-ready-to-hand and of existence. The sentence then says: Being as existence is not itself the existent being; being as being-ready-to-hand is not itself the ready-to-hand being. Whereas existence stands in that essential relation to the one existing, according to which existence determines the existing one as such and according to which it is that on the basis of which the existing one has always already been understood, it is, *as that which determines thus* and *as that on the basis of which understanding* [takes place], essentially *different* from the existing being. Moreover: Whereas being-ready-to-hand stands in such an essential relation to the ready-to-hand being – according to which it determines this as such a one and simultaneously is that on the basis of which what is ready-to-hand is always already understood – as that which so determines and as that on the basis of which understanding [takes place], it is essentially different from the ready-to-hand being.

For the understanding comportment to beings as being-ready-to-hand, being – both what is own in the way of existence and the being of non-human beings as being-ready-to-hand – is understood in advance. Being as existence and being as being-ready-to-hand are *disclosed*, that is, opened up, in my twofold understanding of being. Being's being-understood in the *understanding* of being means: *Disclosure* as opening-up of being. The disclosure as openness is the way *own* to being, in which [way] there is being. If the *being* of beings is the thematic object of phenomenological philosophy, then it is *only* as *disclosure of being*. Hence there is being as existence only as disclosure of existence; likewise there is being-ready-to-hand only as disclosure of being-ready-to-hand.

Understanding (disclosure) of own being as existence and understanding (disclosure) of being-ready-to-hand – how do both [141] stand together? In this way: My existence in itself includes the understanding of it itself as well as the understanding of being-ready-to-hand. This twofold understanding of being keeps within an *allocation*, to such an extent that I am disclosed as self-related in my being as existence, as that which my being involves me in my being, but that in this self-related disclosure of my being I *am extended* into the disclosure of being-ready-to-hand. We thus call the disclosure in which my own being as existence is held: the self-related-extended *disclosure*, or the *self-related-ecstatic disclosure*. The disclosure of being-ready-to-hand (and generally the being of non-human beings), into which I in my self-related-ecstatic disclosure am stretched, we designate as *horizonal disclosure*. The self-related-ecstatic and the horizonal disclosure form an unbreakable unity and whole. Thus we speak also of the *holistic disclosure* and distinguish within it the self-related-ecstatic and the horizonal disclosure.

The whole of this self-related-ecstatic-horizonal disclosure of being is in essence that which Heidegger refers to in the appellation "Dasein." Indeed, we read in *Being and Time* that the *entity* that we ourselves always are is terminologically grasped as *Dasein*,[385] whereas the [way of] *being* itself, "to which Dasein can comport itself in this way or that and always somehow does comport itself," is called *existence*.[386] This terminological determination has been understood many times to the effect that what is thematized existentially-ontologically as Dasein is initially only the existing being in its existence. And Heidegger does say that with the appellation "Dasein" the beings that exist are designated, and with the expression "existence" the being of these beings is designated. However, he adds that the appellation "Dasein" "is chosen as a pure expression of being."[387] The being that I myself am and that is not like other beings that are ready-to-hand or present-at-hand, but rather exists, gets the ontological designation "Dasein," because, in the self-related-ecstatic disclosure of its existence, [142] it is disclosed-stretched into the horizonal disclosure of the ways of being of beings that are not Dasein. The word element "-sein" in the appellation "Da-sein" means being as existence, whereas the word element "Da-" means the *whole* disclosure, not only the disclosure of being as existence, but rather *with it* the disclosure of ways of being of all beings that are not Dasein. The whole disclosure is opened up to the extent that I in my self-related-ecstatic disclosure (existence) am stretched into the horizonal disclosure (being of beings that are not Dasein).

Let us return to Heidegger's phenomenological concept of phenomenon. If the answer to the fourfold question, with respect to which the formal concept of phenomenon is deformalized to the phenomenological, is that it is the *being* of beings that is hidden in every self-showing of beings – but as so hidden belongs to the self-showing of beings as their sense and ground – *then* the "hidden being" is only the terminological condensation for that which we have just established as the whole disclosure of being, in itself organized self-relatedly-ecstatically and horizonally. In the self-showing of beings – in the natural as well

---

385 Ibid., 10 & 16; EA, 7 & 11.
386 Ibid., 16; EA, 12.
387 Ibid., 17; EA, 12.

as positivist-scientific self-showing – the whole disclosure of being remains hidden and veiled. If *as* disclosure it is to become the being of the *phenomenon*, that is, if it is to be *brought* to self-showing-in-itself, it must be *explicitly unveiled* through the logos of phenomenology. Because there is being only in its disclosure, because the disclosure of ways of being of beings that are not Dasein is opened up as the horizon for the self-related-ecstatic disclosure of my existence, and because the self-related-ecstatic disclosure of my existence (and its existentials)[388] in unity with its horizonal disclosure makes up the *full sense of Dasein*, the philosophical thematization of the being of beings and of the sense of being must be exposed as *existential analytic of Dasein*. This is enacted as the step-by-step unveiling of the self-related-ecstatic-horizonal disclosure of being in general.

(β) Husserl's Deformalization of the Formal Concept
      of Phenomenon in the Direction of the Pure, viz.,
      Transcendental Life of Consciousness

In an earlier place in our considerations we said: Commonality between the Husserlian and Heideggerian understanding of phenomenology consists in that which Heidegger establishes as the *formal* concept of phenomenology, which in principle coincides with Husserl's formal evidence-concept – to the extent that it is expressed by the maxim "to the things themselves!" Seen from the perspective of Heidegger's asking the question of the deformalization of the formal to the phenomenological phenomenon-concept, the *difference from Husserl* breaks open when one is brought before this question: With respect to what is Husserl's formal concept of phenomenon to be deformalized to the phenomenological concept of phenomenon? The thematic object of Husserlian phenomenology is the *life of consciousness* with its *lived-experiences*, namely, *acts*, and with that which in the acts of consciousness is *given objectively in consciousness*. If what is named here is to be phenomenon in the phenomenological sense – and that means in the philosophical and not only in the ordinary sense – then it must *also* be

---

388 [Translator's note: *Existenzialien* – here translated as "existentials" – is to be understood within the framework of *Existenz* (and has nothing to do with what we normally mean by existentialism). In this framework the existentials are ontological aspects of the being of Dasein as *Existenz*. Cf. Glossary in "Translator's Introduction."]

something that does *not* show itself in the natural as well as the positivist-scientific self-showing of beings, that is hidden and veiled therein, but as so veiled also somehow is ground for the natural and positivist-scientific self-showing of beings. As so veiled, it then also needs, essentially and necessarily, an explicit showing and unveiling, which is also distinct from the positivist-scientific showing.

But is it not my I with its life of consciousness, its manifold lived-experiences and acts of perceiving, remembering, expecting, or judging, along with the objects of my lived-experiences, that always already and without explicit phenomenological showing shows itself to me? Am I not the one who in every moment of its waking life of consciousness is given to it itself, in the manifold lived-experiences of consciousness? Is it not the objects of my lived-experiences of consciousness that always already show themselves to me in my natural life of consciousness? One has to agree with all of that, but at the same time one has also to say contrarily [144] that, in *that* way in which I am always already opened to me myself in my life of consciousness, this is *not* to become thematic object of the phenomenology of consciousness. In the introduction to the second volume of *Logical Investigations*, Husserl says programmatically: "The source of all difficulties lies in the unnatural direction of intuition and thinking that is demanded in phenomenological analysis. Instead of arising in *enactment* of the manifold acts that build one on the other, and thus positing the objects that are meant in their sense, so to speak, naively as beings ... we should rather 'reflect,' i.e., make these acts themselves and their immanent sense-content into objects."[389] In the *natural* enactment of consciousness we live in our acts in such a way that we *live through them unthematically*, are absorbed in them, and are directed thematically only to the objects that are meant in the acts. It belongs to the experience of the acts that is lost to self that we naively suppose the objects of our acts, to which we are expended as perceiving, remembering, or wishing, to be beings, that is, as *present-at-hand beings that are independent of act*.

In this natural self-showing of me myself (in this natural self-givenness) and the objects of my lived-experiences, there remains something hidden, which can only be unveiled through a proper *reflection*. In this reflection I retract myself from my being expended in experiencing acts to the objects that are naively posited as beings and *bend* my thematizing

---

389   Husserl, *Logische Untersuchungen*, II/1, 9; *Huss.*, XIX/1, 14; ET, 255.

view *back*, objectifying, to the acts that otherwise remain unthematic. What phenomenological reflection shows through the phenomenological attitude of thinking – what shows itself ordinary as what is hidden of the naive act-enactment, which thus *becomes phenomenon* – this is the *pure essence of acts* and their *essential relationship to objects*. In this phenomenological research-attitude the acts of consciousness show themselves in their general and specific essence. Their general essence is contained in their *intentionality*. Intentionality says that every act of consciousness is essentially a relating-to-something and not just on the basis of the accidental surfacing of [145] objects. The specific essence of the acts means that, in accord with its type of essence, every type of act relates to *its* object: the perceiving act making present to a corporeally present thing, the recollecting act making present to a corporeally present-past.

The phenomenological discovery of intentionality as what essentially constitutes lived-experiences of consciousness includes the essential insight that the objects of lived-experience are not simple, as in the natural life of consciousness; rather, they are as that which they are known for me only in the *intentional immanence* of consciousness: immanent as that which they are meant in the acts and depending on the type of essence of the acts. We only become intentionally conscious of – that is, perceive or remember – the objects of sense experience to the extent that they present themselves in various ways in the acts that mean them, that is, *appear* in them. Husserl also relates the word *phenomenon* specifically back to the Greek φαινόμενον and translates the word as "what appears"[390] [*das Erscheinende*]; but he does not think of "what appears" as appearance in the sense in which Heidegger differentiates it from what shows itself; rather, he takes it precisely in the meaning of what shows itself. In accord with the intentional difference between consciousness-act and act-object, Husserl distinguishes between what appears (as act-object) and its appearing, that is, its ways of appearing in the acts of consciousness.

(γ) The Phenomenological Phenomena of
    Husserl and Those of Heidegger

The phenomena of Husserl's phenomenology are the whole of my subjective life of consciousness – unveiled and thematized in the

---

390 Husserl, *Die Idee der Phänomenologie*, 14; ET, 11.

phenomenological attitude of thinking – in its intentionally constituted lived-experiences and in the objects known intentionally therein. The deciding question now reads: In what relationship do the phenomeno-logical [146] phenomena named by Husserl stand to the phenomeno-logical phenomena of Heidegger? *How do the phenomena of consciousness stand in relationship to the phenomena of Dasein?*

In order to achieve a landmark for a comparative contrast, one must say initially that what for Husserl are *intentionally* constituted *lived-experiences of consciousness* are for Heidegger the *comportments of Das-ein*. Husserl's phenomenological thematization of the intentional acts is from Heidegger's formulation of the question a philosophical analysis of the comportments. This reveals what in the acts remains hidden in the *pre*-philosophical, naive act-enactment. But for Heidegger the acts as comportments are those wherein I am given to me myself as a self-related being: *pre*-phenomenological in the mode of the self-forgetting living-through, phenomenological in the mode of revealing thema-tization. Life in my intentional comportments, however, is *ontic* self-givenness, *not* the *being* of my self in the ontological difference from me as the self-related being. What lies at the *basis* of my ontic self-givenness in my intentional comportments is the still hidden disclosure of my being as existence. Therefore for Heidegger, showing-revealing of the self-related-ecstatic disclosure of my existence belongs to the *primary* theme of phenomenological philosophy.

When Heidegger designates that which Husserl calls lived-experience or act as comportment, the issue is not only about a different use of lan-guage. The basis for the other terminological designation lies in the fun-damentally other interpretation and determination of this phenomenon, namely hermeneutic and not reflective. One of the most important *the-matic* links of Heidegger to Husserl is Heidegger's positive assessment of Husserl's phenomenological insight into intentionality. Therefore for Heidegger the comportments of Dasein, the ways of dealing-with and going-around-with, are essential ways of the self's relating to that with which I deal and in which I am engaged, and therefore intentionally constituted. The teaching of intentionality is for Heidegger a first and deciding step on the way of abandoning the teaching of the "inner" do-main of the subject, which first must be transcended for every connect-ing to world. But when Heidegger gives expression to this phenomenon itself positively and indeed hermeneutically, he refrains from speaking of acts of consciousness, but also of intentionality of comportment. In-stead, he speaks of *"being-amidst-innerworldly-things."* Therefore, if

Heidegger grasps the phenomenon that Husserl determines as intentional act of consciousness, as intentional comportment – and this as being-with-beings – then he roots the intentionality of comportment back into the being-constitution of self-comporting Dasein. Of course the self-comporting being-with-beings is not itself the constitution of being. But it is the way in which Dasein, on the *basis* of its ecstatic being-constitution itself, *is being with* being to which it comports itself as self-comporting being.

Being-with of comportments is according to its way of being *concern*. The concernful being-with-beings is in itself a twofold phenomenon: a founded and a founding one. Up to now we have aimed our look only at the founded phenomenon: the concernful comportment within which Dasein is itself a being. The *taking root* of "intentionality" of concernful comportment in the ecstatic existence is the *founding* of the *ontic*-concernful comportment in the *ecstatic*-concernful being-with. As existential, this concernful being-with forms, along with the existentials of throwness and throwing-open, the whole of ecstatic existence, which Heidegger designates terminologically as *care*. As care, Dasein is in-itself-ecstatically disclosed in the three ecstasies of throwing-open, throwness, and the ecstatic being-with [*Entwurf, Geworfenheit, ekstatisches Sein-bei*]. To grasp the *ontic intentionality* from out of the *ecstatic being-constitution* of Dasein means to understand it as ontic-concernful being with concerned-for beings and to unveil the ontic concern in its foundedness in the self-related-ecstatic disclosure of ecstatic being-with in unity with ecstatic throwing-open and ecstatic throwness. Their unveiling is the *primary* theme of phenomenology, because it is only from out of the self-related-ecstatic disclosure of the ecstatic [148] constitution of care that the ontic-intentional self-relating to beings can be clarified.

Husserl's phenomenological thematization of how the intentional object variously *appears* in the acts of consciousness is from Heidegger's point of view the philosophical analysis of *comportment-related self-showing* of beings. The how of the appearance of the intentional object in the acts of consciousness (e.g., ways that the aspects appear and the perspectival ways of appearing) is the philosophically thematized self-showing of *beings* – but *not the being* of the self-showing beings that is to be thought from out of the ontological difference from beings. The natural as well as the phenomenologically thematized appearing – which is related both to act and to comportment – and the self-showing of beings take place on the *basis* of the (for the phenomenological thematization of the comportment-related appearing of beings) *veiled disclosure of the be-ing* of appearing beings. The revealing of this *horizonal* disclosure of be-ing, together with the revealing of the self-related-ecstatic disclosure of existence (care), is the *primary* theme of a hermeneutic phenomenology of *Dasein* – in contrast with reflective phenomenology of *consciousness*.

3. Phenomenology as Method of Access to the Thematic Field of Investigation (Second Methodological Principle)

(a) Heidegger's Three Methodological Directives

The reflection on the formal and the phenomenological phenome-non- and phenomenology-concept has presented the phenomenologi-cal method up to now as a *way of treatment*, as an explicitly showing letting-be-seen of that which shows itself in and from itself. However, with that we do not yet know which way the showing letting-be-seen, the logos of phenomenology, must pursue in order *to bring* the self-related-ecstatic-horizonal disclosure of [149] being in general to self-showing-in-itself. The methodological question about the way is the question of *how* we *arrive at* catching sight of the *being* of beings in such a way that we can thematize it specifically [as] being that de-termines beings as beings and whereupon we in our comportment to beings have always already understood this. However, being as what so determines and as the whereupon of understanding conceals itself in the self-showing of beings.

The section of *Being and Time* on methodology also says something decisive about this, even if only in one single sentence. It is in the Mar-burg lecture course *Basic Problems of Phenomenology* (GA 24) that the methodological significance of that sentence is highlighted. To begin with, a sentence precedes this one that once again says something es-sential from the preceding discussion of the way of treatment: "The way of encountering being and the structures of being in the mode of phenomenon must be *reclaimed* from the objects of phenomenology."[391] But then we read: "Therefore the *opening* of the analysis as well as the *ac-cess* to the phenomenon and the *passage through* the reigning occlusions demand their own methodological securing."[392] In the Marburg lecture

---

391 Heidegger, *Sein und Zeit*, 49; EA, 36.
392 Ibid.

course just mentioned, Heidegger discusses *three basic parts* of the *phenomenological method*: phenomenological *reduction*, phenomenological *construction*, and phenomenological *destruction*.[393] What is shown here is that the task of phenomenological securing of the opening of the analysis is taken on by phenomenological reduction, that the task of phenomenological securing of the access to the being-phenomenon is taken on by phenomenological construction, and that the task of phenomenological securing of the passage through the reigning occlusions is taken on by phenomenological destruction.

[150] These three basic parts together reveal – as we can say – the second methodological principle in the shape of *three directives*. We know in the meantime that what Heidegger calls the phenomenological manner of treatment is for Husserl the principle of formal evidence in the sense of the phenomenological research-maxim, which he designates as first methodological principle. We said earlier that the discussion of a first methodological principle calls for a *second one*. As we have just become acquainted with this in the three methodological directives, that which we can designate as second phenomenological principle for Husserl can be said as well as for Heidegger. Husserl designates *his* second methodological principle within transcendental phenomenology as the method of the phenomenological, namely, *transcendental epoché* and *reduction*,[394] to which he also gives the name *fundamental method*.[395] As a second methodological principle, it is the transcendental transmutation of that phenomenological reflection in which I retrieve myself from the naive act-enactment and reflect on the life of the act itself. We dare not equate this reflection with the reflection that makes up Husserl's phenomenological gaze in the sense of the maxim "to the things themselves!"

The fundamental method of epoché and reduction is, similar to Heidegger's three methodological directives, a *method of access*, which methodologically provides access to the respective field of investigation of phenomenology and which *as* method of access is not to be confused with the method of the way of treatment.

---

393 Heidegger, *Die Grundprobleme der Phänomenologie*, GA 24, 26ff.
394 Cf. here Husserl, *Ideen I*, second section, 48ff., esp. 57ff.; *Huss.*, III, 57ff., esp. 69ff.
395 Husserl, *Cartesianische Meditationes*, in *Huss.*, I, 61.

As is shown, within the second methodological principle, both Husserl and Heidegger speak of a *reduction*; but this is in each case with a fundamentally *different* meaning. Both meanings of "reduction" are differentiated, as with reflection and hermeneutic as well as consciousness and Dasein. Common to Husserl's transcendental reduction and to Heidegger's hermeneutic [151] reduction is only their belonging to the phenomenological method of access in its difference from method of the way of treatment.

What does the phenomenological reduction mean for Heidegger?[396] It is the *first* directive for the *revealing way to the being* of beings as the thematic object of phenomenology. Because being is essentially the being *of beings*, the phenomenological analysis must *originate* with beings. With that it must target the beings whose being is to be shown to them in such a way that they show themselves *as determined through the way of being that is own to them*. Simultaneously it must avoid bringing beings to *that* approach for the *opening* of the analysis in a manner of being that covers up their genuine way of being. The task of phenomenological *passage through* the possible occlusions is the critical vigilance that reigns here. Proceeding from beings, the phenomenological view enacts a turning *away from* what are otherwise *only* thematic beings (in the natural as well as scientific-researching access to them) and *back to* the *being* (way of being) of these beings, so that now, in the phenomenological-philosophical attitude, *being* is held in view *thematically*, while *beings* of this being are held in view only *co*-thematically. The fact that the phenomenological analysis of the being of beings in the designated manner must originate from beings means that now even "the ordinary concept of phenomenon {beings}" becomes "phenomenologically relevant."[397] But note: The ordinary phenomenon-concept is *phenomenologically* relevant – that is, for the sake of the revealing of being – and not, for example, positively-scientifically relevant.

In the phenomenological *construction* that follows on the phenomenological reduction, the phenomenological look heads for the being that is only targeted through the reduction, but now *revealing* and grasping it.[398] Thus the talk of *access* [*Zu-gang*] to being as self-showing-in-itself.

---

396 Cf. for the following Heidegger, *Die Grundprobleme der Phänomenologie*, GA 24, 28f.
397 Heidegger, *Sein und Zeit*, GA 2, 49f.; EA, 37.
398 Heidegger, *Die Grundprobleme der Phänomenologie*, GA 24, 29f.

[152] The *third* basic part of the phenomenological method of access, phenomenological *destruction* as critical passage through the misplacing phenomena, now follows after the second, just as the second follows after the first. Because in phenomenological destruction the *critical function* of the phenomenological method is exercised, it accompanies the effort of reduction as well as construction. As phenomenological-critical passage through the misplacings, which cover over the genuine being-phenomena, phenomenological destruction is activated within the systematic outline of *Being and Time* – and not primarily or only in the second part, which has as its task a phenomenological destruction of the history of ontology.[399] On the contrary, the *first* step of executing phenomenological analysis in § 12, which itself still keeps within the limits of the phenomenological reduction, is already accompanied by the critical passage though the misplacing, in which the in-being of Dasein initially shows itself to the self-thematic look.

On the way of reduction and construction, accompanied by the critically functioning destruction, there is disclosed step by step in *Being and Time* the being *of* the being that I myself always am, as the self-related-ecstatic disclosure of my existence and the existentials that form my existence. Likewise the being *of* the being to which I always comport myself as existing being, reveals itself as the horizonal disclosure of ways of being of beings that are not Dasein. On the way of existential-ontological analysis, the self-related-ecstatic disclosure reveals itself as one to whose existential sense belongs being opened and expanded into the horizonal disclosure of being of all beings that are not Dasein.

[153]

(b) Husserl's Fundamental Method

Over against this, what does the transcendental-phenomenological reduction together with the transcendental-phenomenological epoché in Husserl accomplish? Epoché says "holding back" and means just that. According to Husserl, I exercise the phenomenological epoché when I reflectively hold myself back from the positing of present-at-handness, which absorbs my natural life of consciousness and is always already implicitly enacted. In this positing that determines my naive

---

399 Heidegger, *Sein und Zeit*, GA 2, 27ff. & 52f.; EA, 19ff., & 39f.

life of consciousness and my naive enactment of acts, I comprehend the entire world-actuality – both the physical and the psychic actuality that is own to my subjective life of the soul – as being present-at-hand and in this sense being-actual. To this natural and general positing of present-at-handness, which Husserl also calls the general thesis of the natural attitude of consciousness,[400] belongs the self-forgetting and self-concealing living-through of my acts of consciousness and the exclusive living-toward the things of my experiencing, handling, and positivistically-scientifically cognizing psychic life – things that are supposedly pre-given and independent of consciousness, and in this sense posited as ready and present-at-hand.

As reflective holding-back over against this natural-naive general thesis, the transcendental-phenomenological epoché is the *reflective* bending-myself-back *to* the life of consciousness that is otherwise lived-through in a concealing fashion and thus unregarded. If in the natural life of consciousness I stand on the natural being-ground of what is present-at-hand that encompasses the world as ob-ject and me myself as subject, then I reflectively abandon this natural world-ground through enacting the epoché; reflectively I gain standing in me myself as my transcendental life of consciousness, cleansed of the natural positing of present-at-handness. Through the reflective effort of the transcendental epoché, my phenomenological look is led-back (reduced) to my pure life of consciousness in its essential correlation of the intentionally constituted pure acts of consciousness and intentional-immanent act-objects. [154] This correlation, involving the whole of transcendental life of consciousness, is the *connection of act-like ways of appearing to the appearing intentional objects* in the ways of appearance.

For Husserl the method of access of the transcendental epoché and reduction performs the revealing uncovering of the *absolute being* of pure consciousness. This being is called absolute because it bears within itself the other type of being, reality as the being of the spatial-temporal world, as intentional sense.[401] But seen from Heidegger's basic hermeneutic position, the reductively opened absolute being of consciousness is *not* the *genuine way of being* of the "subject." Rather, in the reductive access to the absolute domain of being, the "subject" is grounded in itself as the transcendental *ego-cogito-cogitatum* and once

---

400 Husserl, *Ideen I*, 52; *Huss.*, III, 62f.
401 Ibid., 91ff. & 53ff.; *Huss.*, III, 114ff. & 118f.

and for all closes itself off from the possibility of hermeneutic revealing of its existential constitution of being and of the self-related-ecstatic-horizonal disclosure of being in general.

§ 4. Hermeneutic and Reflective Logos

The designation of the preliminary concept of phenomenology in section C of § 7 of *Being and Time* ends with the determination of phenomenology as *hermeneutics*.[402] What follows as the final step is, sure enough, to be understood in such a way that all previously taken steps in the determination of the phenomenological method were enacted as those of *hermeneutic* phenomenology and, looking back, must be understood as such. Our presentation of the phenomenological method of *Being and Time* was oriented to the differentiation between the phenomenological way of treatment as the first phenomenological principle, and the phenomenological method of access as the second. Way of treatment and method of access must therefore [155] be recognized as principles of *hermeneutics*. Hermeneutics, as Heidegger worked it out for the first time and fundamentally in the war emergency semester course, is differentiated from reflection and theory in the sense just elucidated. The hermeneutic way of treatment and the hermeneutic method of access are a-theoretical and a-reflective methodological principles. Over against that, the way of treatment and method of access in Husserl's phenomenology have a theoretical-reflective nature. Thus it is a question of differentiating Heidegger's phenomenological way of treatment and method of access in its *hermeneutic* character from Husserl's phenomenological way of treatment and method of access in its *reflective* character.

Up to now the logos of phenomenology – in sections B and C of § 7 of *Being and Time* – was determined as "showing and revealing letting-be-seen." What the logos allows to be seen in showing and revealing is what-shows-itself-in-itself, the phenomenon. The showing and revealing letting-be-seen enacts the sense of phenomenological description. In the showing and revealing letting-be-seen, Heidegger takes up phenomenological intuition. The showing and revealing, intuitive letting-be-seen, the logos of phenomenology, is enacted either reflectively, as

---

402 Heidegger, *Sein und Zeit*, GA 2, 50f.; EA, 37ff.

with Husserl, or hermeneutically, as with Heidegger. The formal concept of phenomenology as it is established by Heidegger is, as formal, neutral over against the possible shapings of reflective or hermeneutic phenomenology.

Now, in order to emphasize the hermeneutic character of phenomenology, in section C of § 7 of *Being and Time*, first of all "the methodological sense of phenomenological description"[403] is grasped as "interpretation [*Auslegung*]." That means: The logos of phenomenology is enacted as showing and revealing letting-be-seen as *interpretation*. The showing and revealing letting-be-seen, the phenomenological description of what shows itself in and from itself in this letting-be-seen, is interpretation.

It is true that reflective letting-be-seen, the reflective showing and revealing, [156] *can* be understood and designated as interpretation. In that the reflecting act refers to the act that was lived-through earlier but is now an ob-jectifying act – to the making present of the lived-experience of consciousness – it interprets this step by step with regard to what constitutes it. Interpretation can also be reflection, if it is designated as reflection. Reflection can also be grasped as interpretation, an interpretation that takes place in the reflective approach. Stepping out of the living-through of the lived-experience, the turn of the I-look from the lived object back to the living-experience of this object – this belongs to this specifically meant reflection. Through this reflective turning of the I-look, the reflected lived-experience becomes intentional object of the lived-experience of reflection. The distance of reflecting observation is formed between the reflecting act and the ob-jectifying lived-experience. The reflectively observed and theoretically ob-jectified lived-experience is located in the over-against of the one who is reflecting theoretically. Here the interpretation of the reflectively observed lived-experience of consciousness is enacted from out of the reflective distance from the lived-experience to be interpreted.

Of course, when Heidegger designates the methodological sense of phenomenological description as *interpretation*, this designation is already carried out in dissociation from the methodological sense of phenomenological description as reflection. In order to make this non-reflective sense of interpretation terminologically and unambiguously

---

403 Ibid., 50; EA, 37.

differentiated from reflection, interpretation is grasped as ἑρμηνεύειν. The methodological sense of phenomenological showing and revealing, that is, description, is not reflective, but rather *hermeneutic interpretation*. What appears to be a pleonasm is in truth the unambiguous determination of what alone is meant by interpretation: not the reflective but the a-reflective interpretation. Insofar as phenomenology here is not that of consciousness but rather that of Dasein, "the λόγος of the phenomenology of Dasein ... [has] the character of ἑρμηνεύειν."[404] Just as the hermeneutic phenomenology [157] of the a-theoretical domain of life and of lived-experience begins with the interpreting understanding of the lived-experience of the surrounding world, so too does the hermeneutic phenomenology of pre-theoretical Dasein begin with the interpreting understanding of pre-theoretical comportments to the surrounding world and to beings in the surrounding world (tools). The interpreting understanding does not bring the comportments to be interpreted into the opposite of an object of reflection, but rather remains for the interpretation in the enactment of the comportment that is untouched in reflection and goes along with its enactment-direction, even if in the mode of explicitness. In this mode of explicitness the interpreting understanding makes explicit the comportment as such and the whereunto of this comportment, in such a way that the comportment shows itself as involvement-with and the whereby of the involvement as what is each time determined as involvement (what is significant). With that the hermeneutic starting-situation is outlined for the hermeneutic uncovering of the ownmost way of being of comportments, namely, of ways of involvement as well as the primary constitution of being of involved-determined beings (of the surrounding world). The hermeneutic-ontological showing of the way of being and the constitution of being also takes place in *going-along with* the enactment-direction of a-theoretical ways of involvement.

Interpretation as ἑρμηνεύειν, as hermeneutics, is determined in three intertwining respects. Through ἑρμηνεύειν "the genuine sense of being and the basic structures of its own being are *announced* to the understanding of being that belongs to Dasein itself."[405] Hermeneutic phenomenology of Dasein is the explicitly hermeneutic self-interpretation

---

404 Ibid.
405 Ibid.

of the understanding of being that belongs to Dasein, with respect to its universal expanse. The self-interpretation of the understanding of being is self-announcement. The hermeneutic (not reflective) interpreting is an announcing, a giving of tidings, of what implicitly comprises the universal understanding of being that is enacted by Dasein. In this giving of tidings the implicitly enacted understanding of being is raised step by step into explicitness and explicit transparency. But here it is all about seeing that this [158] phenomenological self-interpretation as self-announcing is not enacted in the attitude of reflection, but rather in the attitude of hermeneutics. This hermeneutic attitude must be taken up knowingly and in full transparency. For it is only from out of this hermeneutic attitude that the series of steps of all parts of the analyses of the Dasein-analytic is carried out.

When it is said of the hermeneutic logos of "phenomenology of Dasein" that through it "the actual sense of being and the basic structures of its own being" are revealed to the understanding of being that belongs to Dasein, then it becomes clear, through the naming of the "actual sense of being" together with the "phenomenology of Dasein," that this includes not only – as is mostly presumed – the analytic of Dasein in the narrower sense (first and second section of the first part of Being and Time), but also the uncovering of the horizonal temporality of beings that are not Dasein (third section under the title "Time and Being"). But that says that in the appellation "Dasein" not only the essence (being) of human being is indicated, but also the belonging-together of the transcending existence with the horizonally disclosed temporal sense of being that is not that of Dasein. All three sections of the first part of Being and Time make up fundamental ontology. Fundamental ontology taken as a whole – that is, in its three steps of preparatory fundamental analysis, of the uncovering of the being-sense of existence that understands being, and of the explication of the horizonal temporality [Temporalität] of the being that is not Dasein's, which belongs to existential temporality [Zeitlichkeit] – is accomplished as hermeneutics, as hermeneutic phenomenology.

The self-interpretation and the self-announcing of "the actual sense of being" is what is first named as thematic of hermeneutic phenomenology of Dasein, although this is not the first but the third step of hermeneutics. But the self-announcing of the actual sense of being (of beings that are not Dasein) is not what is carried out first because the self-announcing of "the basic structure of its own being," named in the second place, [159] is directed toward the answer to the basic question of the sense of being in general, that is, the interpretation of the temporal sense of being of beings that are not Dasein. "Phenomenology of Dasein" in the broad sense, which under the title "Time and Being" includes the answer to the basic question of the sense of being in general, is "*hermeneutic* in the originary meaning of the word, according to which it designates the business of interpretation."[406] The phenomenology of Dasein in the whole of its three steps is hermeneutics – and not reflection. But hermeneutics here always means hermeneutic phenomenology in contrast to reflective phenomenology. Phenomenology of Dasein is hermeneutics, and hermeneutics is phenomenology of Dasein. For determining the sense of hermeneutics, that is, of that which here in the context of the phenomenology of Dasein says hermeneutics and hermeneutic, it is not sufficient to revert to the older history of hermeneutics and its origin. For all shapes of the older hermeneutics are determined through the explicit and implicit domination of the theoretical, of which it says in the war emergency semester course that it must be sundered, if we are to be able to penetrate into the so far undiscovered region of the a-theoretical. To the region of the a- and pre-theoretical, however, belongs the hermeneutic of the phenomenology of Dasein. The hermeneutic as method emerges from the primordial experience of the region of the a-theoretical, and indeed in such a way that insight into the a-theoretical sketches out the basic trait of hermeneutics as methodological way of treatment of and methodological access to the a-theoretical. What simply appears – hermeneutics as the business of interpretation – is in truth a basic methodological attitude that must be practised first, because as scientific method it is neither reflection nor theory.

As hermeneutics, the phenomenology of Dasein is itself a-theoretical and a-reflective. But the a-theoretical and the a-reflective hermeneutic is the scientific and as such the phenomenological method from the region of a-theoretical Dasein.

[160] But the hermeneutic logos of the phenomenology of Dasein is in itself both hermeneutic way of treatment and hermeneutic way of access. The hermeneutic of the phenomenological way of treatment says that the showing letting-be-seen in the non-reflective attitude is the explicit interpreting of what-shows-itself-in-itself. What-shows-itself-in-itself

---

406 Ibid.

in the opening-situation of hermeneutic phenomenology of Dasein are the ways of comportment of involvement-with as well as the whereby of this involvement – and from here on, the ways of being of concern that are ownmost to the ways of involvement as well as the constitution of the being of the whereby of the involvement as relevance and readiness-to-hand. As phenomenological way of treatment, the logos of phenomenology of Dasein is a hermeneutic letting-be-seen of the phenomena, that is, of that which shows itself in this letting-be-seen ordinary and from it itself.

As phenomenological manner of access, the logos of phenomenology of Dasein is hermeneutic reduction, hermeneutic construction, and hermeneutic destruction. Whereas the phenomenological reduction for Husserl is of a reflective nature, for Heidegger the phenomenological reduction takes place hermeneutically. The turning of the phenomenological look *away from* only thematically innerworldly beings and *back to* the constitution of being that is understood nonthematically in pre-phenomenological understanding of being – this is accomplished in the hermeneutic *going-along with* the comportment of involvement and not in a reflection on the comportment. The phenomenological reduction as the first way-directive for the phenomenology of Dasein is the first step on the hermeneutic way to the – to be thematized – constitution of being of the whereby of the involvement. It is the first step toward explicit thematization of the constitution of being. But at the same time the hermeneutic reduction is the first step on the way to the – to be thematized – way of being of the comportment of involvement. In this first step the comportment of involvement that is accomplished in life is itself made transparent to the way of being that determines it. The hermeneutic-phenomenological reduction accomplishes, in its correlative execution, the first step of making explicit what is [161] accomplished and understood pre-phenomenologically, indeed with aliveness but inexplicitly. The explicitness and transparency, into which the otherwise unexplicit and not thematically transparent is lifted, is of hermeneutic and not reflective nature.

The second phenomenological way-directive within the phenomenology of Dasein is hermeneutic-phenomenological *construction*. It *reveals* what the hermeneutic reduction has at first only targeted as revealable. The hermeneutic construction reveals concern, as ownmost way of being of the comportment of involvement, as well as the constitution of the being of involvement and ready-to-handness, as primary constitution of the being of the whereby of the involvement. When, on the further way of the hermeneutic of Dasein, it becomes manifest that the fundamental character of the being (existence) of Dasein is thrown throwing-open, the being-revealing phenomenological construction can be grasped as hermeneutic throwing-open. For throwing-open says revealing, exposing, opening-up. The thinking of hermeneutic phenomenology shows itself as hermeneutic throwing-open in its difference from phenomenological reflection of the phenomenology of consciousness. The hermeneutic-phenomenological construction is the second step on the way of the hermeneutic explicating of what in pre-phenomenological enactment of Dasein is understood unexplicitly, even if with aliveness.

The third phenomenological way-directive for the phenomenology of Dasein, phenomenological destruction, is also of hermeneutic and not reflective essence. As a critical going-through the misplacing phenomena, it accompanies hermeneutic reduction as well as hermeneutic construction. It prevents a comportment in the surrounding world – that becomes phenomenon not from out of going-along with its direction of enactment but rather from out of reflection on it – from being brought into the hermeneutic approach. Correlatively, hermeneutic destruction prevents the whereby of the comportment of involvement from being brought into the approach as perceptual thing and not as what is significant in the surrounding world. The critical difference between the true and the misplacing phenomenon, between phenomenon and semblance within [162] the hermeneutic-phenomenological analysis, keeps within the hermeneutic attitude, just as do reduction and construction. Destruction, too, accomplishes its vigilant differentiation in the hermeneutic going-along with the comportments of involvement, but not in reflecting on these.

But since for Husserl the phenomenological method moves essentially and only in acts of reflection – with the phenomenological way of treatment of evidence, with the principle of all principles, with the research-maxim "returning to the things themselves" – the phenomenological method of access, the fundamental method, is also of a reflective nature. Phenomenological epoché and reduction are of a reflective nature. As such, this method of access leads back to the pure, transcendental life of consciousness, to transcendental subjectivity. But where the phenomenological reduction, together with phenomenological construction and destruction, has hermeneutic character, it leads the hermeneutic-phenomenological look back to Dasein in its understanding of being.

The phenomenology of Dasein is accomplished as hermeneutic, which now means hermeneutic reduction, hermeneutic construction, and hermeneutic destruction. As hermeneutic construction it reveals step by step the basic existential structures of existence, that is, of the being from Da-sein, the Da, disclosure, not only of existence and its existential structures, but the Da of ways of being that are not of Dasein and the temporal sense of these ways of being. All uncoverings along this way are showings and revealings and as such hermeneutic (and not reflective) revealings. The first and guiding meaning of hermeneutics is the self-interpretation of existing understanding of being with respect to the basic structures of the being of Dasein and of the sense of being of types of being that are not Dasein. In short, hermeneutics says first of all: Phenomenology of Dasein in its expanse as fundamental ontology.

But the hermeneutic revealing of the basic structures of being of Dasein and of the temporal sense of being of ways of being that are not of Dasein now forms the "horizon ... for every further [163] investigation of beings that are not of Dasein."[407] The latter is the task of regional ontologies, themselves grounded in fundamental ontology, or of meta-ontologies[408] of the different regions of beings. With a view to the fundamental-ontological task of grounding, hermeneutics as phenomenology of Dasein (first meaning) is simultaneously "hermeneutics" in the sense of working out the conditions for the possibility of every ontological investigation."[409] Hermeneutics in the first and foundational meaning is simultaneously "hermeneutics" in the second meaning: the working out of the conditions for the possibility of every ontological investigation of regions of beings.

The third meaning of hermeneutics results from the fact that hermeneutics in the first, broad sense is accomplished "as interpretation of the being of Dasein,"[410] before it can segue to revealing the sense of being of ways of beings that are not Dasein. Hermeneutics as "interpretation of the being of Dasein" receives "a specifically third sense, the philosophically understood *primary* sense of an analytic of existentiality of existence."[411] The specifically third sense of hermeneutics is the

---

407 Ibid.
408 Heidegger, *Metaphysische Anfangsgründe der Logik im Ausgang von Leibniz*, GA 26, 199–202.
409 Heidegger, *Sein und Zeit*, GA 2, 50; EA, 37.
410 Ibid.; EA, 38.
411 Ibid.

philosophically "primary" sense, because hermeneutic phenomenology in general *starts* as hermeneutic analytic of the existentiality of existence (first and second section of the first part of *Being and Time*). Hermeneutics in the third but primary sense is the first stretch of the way of the whole of phenomenology, namely, hermeneutic of Dasein, including the revealing of the temporal sense of being of ways of being that are not Dasein. But that simultaneously and yet again emphasizes not only that hermeneutics and hermeneutic phenomenology is the analytic of Dasein in the narrower sense of the analytic of existentiality of existence, [164] but also that hermeneutic phenomenology is fundamental ontology in the whole of its thematic. Beyond that, hermeneutics, which always means hermeneutic phenomenology, is also the philosophical method of regional ontologies, that is, of meta-ontologies – that is, the ontological interpretations of the regions of beings. Hermeneutic phenomenology is the method of philosophy as a whole.

With a view to what Dilthey calls hermeneutics, we read in the end: "In this hermeneutics {as analytic of the existentiality of existence}, insofar as it works out ontologically the historical character [*die Geschichtlichkeit*] of Dasein as the ontic condition for the possibility of historiography [*Historie*], is rooted that which can be called 'hermeneutics' only in a derived way: the methodology of the historical [*historische*] human sciences."[412] The existential analytic of the way of being of history [*Geschichtlichkeit*], which says that Dasein lives historically from within its possibilities of being-in-the-world, is the ontic – in accord with Dasein – but at the same time the ontological – in accord with being – for the possibility of the development of historiography [*Historie*] and historical sciences.

In the second-to-last paragraph of the section in *Being and Time* on methodology, Heidegger sets the following investigations of hermeneutic phenomenology of Dasein into relationship with Husserl's investigations of reflective phenomenology of consciousness: "The following investigations became possible only on the foundation that E. Husserl laid, with whose *Logical Investigations* phenomenology made its breakthrough."[413] The following investigations of *Being and Time* are indeed phenomenological – not reflective but hermeneutic. They

---

412 Ibid.
413 Ibid., 51; EA, 38.

are hermeneutic-phenomenological investigations, not of consciousness but of Dasein. Still, these hermeneutic investigations were made possible only on the foundation that Husserl laid, above all in *Logical Investigations* – on the foundation of reflective-phenomenological [165] investigations of consciousness. Among Husserl's phenomenological works, Heidegger gives priority to this path-breaking work of phenomenology, because, although it is also set reflectively, it does not enact the return to the self-certainty of the Cartesian *ego–cogito–cogitatum* and does not yet enact the link to Kant's critical idealism. In *Logical Investigations*, phenomenology is still carried out in the narrower sense and does not take a position. The analyses of the *Logical Investigations* allowed and still allow the exercise of phenomenological seeing and looking in the purest manner. Without this phenomenological seeing in the reflective attitude, the phenomenological seeing in the hermeneutic attitude would not have been able to unfold.

But to the foundation that Husserl laid in the *Logical Investigations* belongs – besides the methodological aspect of phenomenology – also and at least something that is thing-like: intentionality. In the first Marburg lecture course *Introduction to Phenomenological Research* (WS 1923–4), Heidegger says to this point: "With this discovery of intentionality, for the first time in the whole history of philosophy the way is explicitly given for a radical ontological research."[414] And a little later we read:

> Phenomenology is precisely not directed at acts in the old sense, but rather at the entirely new domain, at the way of self-referencing-to, in such a way that the whereunto of the self-relating is present. As long as I do not have this foundation, I am incapable of seeing, in any sense whatever within direct observation of beings, anything like a being-character – well, of doing anything like ontology. So I come back to the fact that here indeed for the first time in the history of philosophy the foundation for an ontological research is established, in such a way that one can make progress in the manner of scientific investigation and not in the form of mere reflection.[415]

Even if intentionality was discovered as [166] the essential constitution of consciousness, it is not tied solely to reflectively thematized

---

414 Heidegger, *Einführung in die phänomenologische Forschung*, GA 17, 260.
415 Ibid., 262.

consciousness. If reflective access to life is abandoned in favour of hermeneutic access, then intentionality also shows itself as an essential constitution of Dasein. Here the insight even appears that intentionality belongs primarily to a-theoretical life and Dasein – and only to that extent belongs also to theoretically constituted consciousness. The hermeneutic phenomenology of Dasein begins in fact because it hermeneutically uncovers, in the *intentio* of the comportment of involvement, the way of being of concern and, in the *intentum* of the whereby of involvement, the being-traits of involvement and ready-to-handness.

Looking back to the "elucidations of the preliminary concept of phenomenology,"[416] we read that these have shown "that what is essential to it {phenomenology} does not lie in being *actual* as a philosophical 'direction.' Higher than actuality is *possibility*. The understanding of phenomenology happens solely in embracing it as possibility."[417] What is essential to phenomenology as method does not lie in the actuality of the direction in which Husserl developed phenomenology. It is "direction" in two senses. On the one hand it is philosophical direction to the extent that phenomenology is understood as reflection. On the other hand Husserl's phenomenology *after Logical Investigations* became a philosophical direction, because it unfolded as transcendental philosophy and phenomenological idealism. Both directions, reflection and idealism in connection with Descartes, Kant, and neo-Kantianism (Natorp), are recognized by Heidegger as constituting the actuality of phenomenology – in which, however, the possibility of phenomenology is not exhausted. Phenomenology as it is understood in the principle of all principles and in the investigation-maxim is primarily "possibility." Higher than every actuality of phenomenology is [167] phenomenology in its character as possibility. To understand phenomenology in its first methodological principle means to understand it in its character as possibility. To understand phenomenology as possibility is to experience that the return to the things themselves can also be enacted in another way than in the one that has become actual. To understand phenomenology as possibility can mean to enact the return to the things themselves, not along the way of reflection but rather along that of hermeneutics. Phenomenology as hermeneutics arises from

---

416 Heidegger, *Sein und Zeit*, GA 2, 51; EA, 38.
417 Ibid.

phenomenology's character as possibility. Heidegger understood phenomenology as a philosophizing from within the things themselves, in seizing phenomenology as possibility, as the possibility of phenomenology that is not reflective but hermeneutic.

In the footnote to this passage, Heidegger says: "If the following investigation makes any steps forward in the disclosure of the 'things themselves,' the author thanks above all E. *Husserl*, who during the author's years as an assistant in Freiburg, through strong personal guidance and through the most liberal lending of unpublished investigations, familiarized the author with the most varied areas of phenomenological research."[418] The investigation goes some steps "forward," insofar as, in encountering Husserl's reflective phenomenology, it saw and comprehended the possibility of a hermeneutic phenomenology. The investigation of *Being and Time* goes some steps "forward," not within reflective phenomenology, but rather by recasting reflective phenomenology to hermeneutic phenomenology. But hermeneutics, too, as phenomenology, remains "disclosure of the 'things themselves.'" As phenomenology it holds fast to the basic principle of returning to the things themselves, only now this return is no longer of a reflective nature, but rather of a hermeneutic nature.

But even the steps "forward," that is, outside reflective phenomenology and as hermeneutic phenomenology of Dasein, [168] are because of Husserl's "strong personal guidance" and of the study of Husserl's unpublished phenomenological investigations. This means that the intensive and broadly applied encounter with the phenomenological analyses of Husserl's reflective phenomenology leads to a secure taking up and carrying out of hermeneutic phenomenology. But that means that those who want to learn the ropes of the hermeneutic phenomenology of Dasein methodically and thematically dare not avoid a study of Husserl's reflective phenomenology. Otherwise they would miss the methodological sense of hermeneutic phenomenology, which is gained from out of the encounter with the methodological sense of reflective phenomenology.

The rigour of Husserl's phenomenological analyses and his yield of philosophical knowledge are admirable. Our achievements with regard to the method of hermeneutic phenomenology should simultaneously show that in it there also reigns a scientific rigour that is not inferior to

---

418 Ibid., 52; EA, 38.

reflective phenomenology. Heidegger's hermeneutic phenomenological analyses in *Being and Time* bring to light a rigour that can match the methodological rigour of Husserl's reflective-phenomenological analyses in *Logical Investigations*. The understanding and co-enactment of the one who lays out and interprets must apply the same methodological rigour in following the hermeneutic way of treatment and method of access.

General Index

interpretation, 52–3, 59, 62, 64, 73,
83, 85, 91, 93–4, 97–8, 102–3, 128,
136–9, 142–3; a-reflective, 137;
hermeneutic, 62, 66, 73, 137; Husserlian, 92, 94, 98, 102; reflective,
66, 73, 136–7; in understanding, 52
intuition, xviii, 5, 34, 68–9, 74, 80–4,
88, 99, 111, 126, 135
in-tuition, xviii, 5, 81–4, 86–9

Kant, I., 144–5

life-world. *See* world
listening, 23–4, 33; drawing out in,
23–5; into, 64
lived-experience, xiv, xix, xxiii–iv,
18–20, 22–80, 84, 87–9, 96, 100,
108, 110, 126–8, 136–7
living-experience, xiv, xix, xxiii–iv,
20–2, 27–9, 34, 41–51, 55–6, 59–62,
66–8, 73–8, 84–9, 101–2, 105, 136
logos, 115, 125, 130, 135–6, 138–40
look, looking, looking-on, xxiii,
5, 12–13, 21–4, 26, 28–9, 31, 45,
55, 72–7, 109, 111–13, 115, 132–3;
I-look, 135–6; into, 33, 41, 46–7,
64–6; out, 111; phenomenological,
132, 134, 140–1, 144

Natorp, P., 145
non-objectifying, 22

objectify, objectification, xix, xxiii–
xxiv, 17, 22, 25, 27–8, 41, 45, 47, 54,
59, 62, 66, 77, 80, 84, 85, 127, 136
ontology, 89, 98–9, 108, 133; fundamental, 138, 142–3

possibility-character, xii, xv,
xvi n, 59, 71, 91–2, 98, 101, 110,
146
principle, 15, 24, 76, 83, 88, 91–2,
102–3, 106–7, 109, 135, 146; of (all)
principles, 79, 80–5, 88, 106, 111,
141, 145; methodological, 107, 112,
115, 130–2, 135, 145; phenomenological, 131–2, 135; *principium*, 15,
81, 83
pro-cess, 23, 28, 42–3, 45–7

reduction, 131–3, 141; eidetic, 98,
100; phenomenological, 131–3,
140–2; transcendental, 100,
131–4, 140
reify, reification, 17, 19, 33

Scheler, M., 110
Sophocles, 44

temporal, temporalizing,
temporality, 19, 27–9, 59, 73, 134,
138–9, 142–3
transcendence, 103

world, worldly, xxiii–xiv, 14, 16–8,
21, 31, 34–6, 40, 42–4, 51–3, 58,
59–61, 63, 65, 67, 89, 93, 102, 105,
128, 134; being-in-the-world, 14,
143; innerworldly, 128, 140; life-
world 14, 18, 21, 31, 52, 63, 102,
105, 116; perceptual, 58; of significance, 40; surrounding, xiv, 14,
22, 29–46, 48–53, 56–67, 73, 88–9,
121, 137, 141; verbal, 14, 40–1, 51,
57, 60, 62

Index of German Words

New Studies in Phenomenology and Hermeneutics

General Editor: Kenneth Maly

Gail Stenstad, *Transformations: Thinking after Heidegger*
Parvis Emad, *On the Way to Heidegger's* Contributions to Philosophy
Bernhard Radloff, *Heidegger and the Question of National Socialism: Disclosure and Gestalt*
Kenneth Maly, *Heidegger's Possibility: Language, Emergence – Saying Be-ing*
Robert Mugerauer, *Heidegger and Homecoming: The Leitmotif in the Later Writings*
Graeme Nicholson, *Justifying Our Existence: An Essay in Applied Phenomenology*
Ladelle McWhorter and Gail Stenstad, eds., *Heidegger and the Earth: Essays in Environmental Philosophy*, Second, Expanded Edition
Richard Capobianco, *Engaging Heidegger*
Peter R. Costello, *Layers in Husserl's Phenomenology: On Meaning and Intersubjectivity*
Friedrich-Wilhelm von Herrmann, *Hermeneutics and Reflection: Heidegger and Husserl on the Concept of Phenomenology*. Translated by Kenneth Maly. Published in German as *Hermeneutik und Reflexion: Der Begriff der Phänomenologie bei Heidegger und Husserl*